SEX GUIDE MASTERY

The Complete Guide To Safe Sex Life, Great Sex For Him And For Her, Awesome Sex Position And Many More.

CHERRY WILSON

Table of Contents

INTRODUCTION...9

    Communication...17

    Acceptance 17

    Relaxation 18

THE SEXUAL ANATOMY...19

    Human Sexual Anatomy as well as Physiology 19

    the minor and significant vestibular glands (VGs). 21

    What is the clitoris? And also, where is it? 22

    Male Anatomy 32

    Sex on the mind 34

SEXUAL REACTION CYCLE...37

    What's the sexual reaction cycle?.................................37

    Which are the phases of this sexual reaction cycle? 37

INDIVIDUAL SEXUAL BEHAVIOR 42

    FORMS OF Activity 45

    ASEXUALITY-Understanding Men's Sexual and Emotional
    Needs 46

    Sexual Behavior OUTSIDE AND INSIDE The Bedroom........49

    Addictive Erotic Behavior...58

FORMS OF SEX OBSESSION "DON'T PERCEIVE IT AS LOVE" 62

    Fantasy Sex 62

    Seductive Purpose Sex 63

Anonymous Sex 63

Spending money on Sex...63

Trading Sex...64

Voyeuristic Sex..64

Exhibitionistic Sex 65

Intrusive Sex..65

Pain Exchange 66

Exploitative Sex 66

The Erotic Pleaser 67

The Sexual Corpse..68

The Sexual Tease...69

SEXUAL HEALTH 72

Pregnancy 74

Birth Control 80

The Importance TO BE Able To Show Yourself Sexually 84

Why ladies love foreplay...87

Why ladies need sexual activity. 89

STAGES OF SEX..91

A Step-By-Step Guide On How To Have Sex 91

When You Have Your Period, Below Are Seven Reasons To Get It On. 98

Hot Easy Ways to great Orgasms!.............................107

THE SEX POSITIONS..110

Best and safe sex position during pregnancy....................110

Shower sex tips 114

Shower sex positions 117

WHAT DO YOU MEAN BY "SMALL"? 123

How To Have Terrific Sex With A Smaller-Than-Average Penis..125

WHAT DO YOU MEAN BY "BIG"? 136

How To Have Great Sex With Bigger-Than-Average Penis 136

If you're having penis-in-vagina sex........................137

If you're having penis-in-anus sex..........................139

Things to remember if you're more gifted................145

If your companion is extra endowed, things to keep in mind 147

EXCELLENT AND ALSO MUCH SAFER SEX...............149

What is a condom? 149

safer Sex..151

SEXUAL DYSFUNCTION 154

DRY PENIS 154

What's to learn about erectile dysfunction? 157

Causes 159

Psychological causes 163

Does operating a bicycle produce ED? 164

Treatment 165

Do health supplements and alternative solutions work? 170

Genital Warts Information, Cause and Chance, Symptoms, Prognosis and Treatment 174

SOME SEXUAL DYSFUNCTION AFFECTING WOMEN 177

Treatment 179

Causes of Fungus Infections................................181

Symptoms of Candida Infection...........................183

Treatments for yeast infection 184

Herpes - Reasons and Therapy 184

PARAPHILLIA 187

What are causes and also threat factors for paraphilia?.........192

SEXUAL TRANSFERRED disease.................................195

What Are STDs? 195

What Triggers Sexually transmitted diseases? 197

Venereal diseases root cause of inability to conceive. 206

Medications for std..208

SEX THERAPY...211

UNDERSTANDING SEX THERAPY 211

SELECTING A SEX THERAPIST 212

WHEN IS SEX THERAPY RECOMMENDED?.....................215

HOW CAN SEX THERAPY HELP? 216

LIMITATIONS AND CONCERNS OF SEX THERAPY 217

CONCLUSION 219

INTRODUCTION

There are many ways at improving sex for couples, but for that to happen, you must first overcome any shyness you may have. Improving sex for couples is about stepping outside your comfort zone and being open to trying new things. If you are overly shy when it comes to sex, you will have difficulties trying to have a better sex life.

Many of us, especially women, are not comfortable with how their bodies look, and this leads to difficulties in the bedroom. Do you find that you only have sex in the dark or you don't ever show yourself naked in front of your partner? This can be a perfect sign that there is some discomfort with body image. Negative body image can make your sex life less enjoyable.

For you to start improving sex for couples, both men and women need to overcome the way that they think about their body. Men and woman come in all sorts of shapes and sizes, and everybody is individual with no two being the same. Sure you can exercise and eat better, we all probably should, but the key to this is coming to terms with your own body. Once you have, you will find that improving sex for couples is much easier and more enjoyable.

Communicate with your partner.

This is another crucial aspect of improving sex for couples. You need to be open and honest with your partner. Discuss any insecurities or bad experiences you may have had, so they have a better understanding of why you act the way you do. Find common ground and work together from there.

If you are shy in the bedroom because you are worried that you are not as experienced as your partner, then you need to tell them. One of the easiest ways of improving sex for couples is to ask your partner to help you by letting them show and tell you what makes them feel good. Let your partner guide you with words and actions.

Never be afraid to say something does not feel right; the point of having sex is to become closer to your partner and enjoy yourself. If something does not feel right tell them and figure out a way around it. No two people have the same sexual preferences but overcoming your shyness and openly communicating about sex is the only way you will start improving sex for couples.

Do you wish that you and your spouse would have hotter sex? Do you want that the two of you could have some more sexual chemistry in the bedroom? Are you tired of hearing all of the feeble excuses that your spouse makes to avoid intimacy with you? Well, it is time that you broke free of all of these problems that you learned more about how to start making love better tonight.

This feeling happens to a lot of married couples, as they grow older together. Most couples lose that sense of passion and desire because they get complacent with one another. You know that this is happening in your relationship and you are determined to put a stop to it. You know that you and your spouse are capable of having amazing sex once again, so you need a little help to make that happen today.

You need to learn all about the useful sex guide. You need to learn some special tip so you can get your spouse in the mood. You need to learn how to make this happen so you can save your marriage and your sanity.

A sex guide for couples can vastly help improve one's sex life, but if you are not capable of active discussing sex with your partner, there is going to be trouble. Many people have a challenging time openly discussing sex with their partners. Hopefully, after reading this, you will have found a way to help open the lines of sexual communication and get on with your sex guide for couples.

Many people have trouble discussing sex, and what happens when they finally get the courage to talk about sex? Things usually end up coming out wrong or not as intended.

One of the first things that you need to do for any sex guide for couples to work is to communicate what you intend to say and ensure that what your partner hears closely matches what you said. We all know what it is like when what you say is very different from what your partner understands.

The simplest way to get over that and ensure that your partner understood what you said is for them to repeat back what you said basically. Agree to let each person speak what is on their mind from start to finish, without interruption. Once they have done so then, the other partner repeats back what they just heard.

Now that may sound simple, but this is not easy to do. You may feel weird at first trying to do this, but after going back and forth a few times, you will be amazed how long it sometimes takes for us to understand what our partner is trying to tell us honestly. Once you have come to an understanding, reverse the roles and let your partner speak while you listen and repeat back.

Once you have learned to improve your sexual communications and start to understand one another, you will find it much more comfortable, and more fun for that matter, to openly explore a sex guide for couples.

Effective communication is the key to any successful relationship. Discover just how much a sex guide for couples can change your sex life.

A great way to start having good sex again tonight is to put the wow factor back into the bedroom. Start pulling out all the stops and go for it. Introduce some new positions that will get you both excited. Trying out new areas is fun, and they bring the two of you closer. Being up against a wall or having the woman on top is much more fun than the traditional missionary position. You need to break away from your comfort zone and start to do a little exploring.

Another way to start making love better tonight is to be the dominant one. Almost every man or woman has the same fantasy of being desired and dominated in the bedroom. We all have this animalistic instinct about us, and we all want to feel that raw passion, but sometimes we are too afraid to take the first step. If you're going to make it happen, then you need to be the one to take the reigns and make the first move. Guaranteed your love life will better from it.

You can make love better if you use this excellent sex guide. You can bring the intimacy back into your relationship full force. Sex is vital to keep your marriage alive, so you need to bring that passion back right now.

A sex guide for couples can aid most improve upon their relationships. If you have been in a relationship for a length of time, you will understand that sex can become routine and even boring. Why? Mostly because we don't know how to introduce sexual variety to our relationships and therefore we don't ever experience great sex while in a marriage or long term relationship.

A sex guide for couples can help us discover how to make sex fresh and exciting again. We all remember what sex was like when a relationship was new. Every time you made love was like a new adventure exploring your partner's body. When we fail to become proactive at improving sex is when sex will become routine.

Routine may be a part of human nature but let's be realistic, it is not how we fantasise our sex lives to be. Having sex in the same place, initiating sex the same way, employing the same foreplay and having the same climax's year after year is how sex becomes routine and is a significant reason why sex becomes less frequent. Discovering a sex guide for couples can be a great way to learn how to break your routine and bring some spice back into your relationship.

Rather than waiting for your relationship to become routine and monotonous, get yourself a useful sex guide for couples and start to proactively and intentionally mix things up. A few helpful tips are:

Start having sex in different places in particular different locations.

Mix up how you have sex. Make foreplay last longer than usual and incorporate different positions.

Men, ensure to give your lady clitoral and g-spot orgasms and varying amounts of each

Introduce sex toys and other props. The number of products on the market place today will keep you on your toes for years.

If you are serious about improving your sex life, get a sex guide for couples and start breaking your mundane routines today. The sooner you do, the sooner you will see your excitement and frequency of sex increase.

Improve the quality of your sex life today. Get yourself a great sex guide for couples and discover what it is like to have fantastic sex

Unfortunately, there is no one magical sex guide for couples, and often these so-called guides do not give you the information want you to want or need. A sex guide is there to help you improve and better your sex life, and there are three things you need to be good at or comfortable with to have a good sex life.

COMMUNICATION

Time and time again, you will run across this all-important word, and it is that important. Proper communication skills are what allows you to let your partner know what feels good and what does not. You need to be able to tell your partner what interests you, what turns you on, and what you are interested in trying. Without proper communication, any sex guide for couples will turn into another paperweight.

ACCEPTANCE

Everyone needs to learn to accept and love their bodies. This is crucial when it comes to having a fulfilling and happy sex life. If you are not satisfied and don't like your organisation, you will never be able to open up and let your partner love your body. Accept and be proud of who you are. Loving yourself first will allow you to give your partner entirely adore you as well.

RELAXATION

Being relaxed around your partner will go a long way in broadening and improving your sex life. If you don't know how to relax, then don't waste time with a sex guide for couples. Learn how to let go and don't worry about your sexual performance too much. By allowing yourself to relax and be in the moment, your sexual performance will take care of itself. Women find it much easier to achieve orgasm if they can relax and enjoy the moment with their partner.

Communication, relaxation and acceptance are three crucial factors to master before any sex guide for couples will work. Once you are comfortable with these, then feel free to experiment. Become a better lover by taking the time to visit Sex4Couples.info. You will learn about some great lovemaking tips, techniques, games and secrets that will help turn your sex life around.

THE SEXUAL ANATOMY

HUMAN SEXUAL ANATOMY AS WELL AS PHYSIOLOGY

It's natural to be interested regarding makeup as well as physiology Being knowledgeable about anatomy as well as physiology enhances our potential for pleasure, physical and also psychological wellness, as well as life satisfaction. Past personal inquisitiveness, thoughtful discussions regarding anatomy and physiology with sexual partners minimise the capacity for miscommunication, unintentional maternities, sexually transferred infections, as well as sex-related dysfunctions. Lastly, and also most significantly, the gratitude of both the biological as well as motivating psychological forces behind sexual curiosity, desire, as well as the capacities of our minds can enhance the health and wellness of relationships.

Possibly the most visible framework of women sexual makeup is the vulva. The main functions of the vulva are a pleasure and also protection. The vulva is composed of the female's external sex organs,

It includes several parts:

(a) the labia majora-- the "big lips" shielding the lady as well as enclosing's internal sex body organs;

(b) the labia minora-- the" tiny lips" bordering as well as defining the openings of the vagina and also urethra;

The clitoris is one of the most delicate erotic zones due to its high focus of nerve endings. By promoting an erotic area, a sex-related physical action can be established right into motion.

The minor VGs-- additionally called Skene's glands (not envisioned), is on the wall of the vaginal area and also are associated with female climaxing, as well as mythologically connected with the G-Spot (Kilchevsky et al., 2012; Wickman, 2017). The major VGs-- also called Bartholin's glands-- lie simply to the left and right of the vagina and also produce lubrication to help in intercourse. Many women-- specifically postmenopausal females-- at some time in their lives report inadequate lubrication, which, consequently, causes discomfort or discomfort throughout sexual relations (Nappi & Lachowsky, 2009). Expanding sexual activity and utilising industrial water-, silicone-, or oil-based personal lubes are necessary remedies to this usual problem.

THE MINOR AND SIGNIFICANT VESTIBULAR GLANDS (VGs).

Feel-good areas: erogenous areas

When boosted, erotic areas are locations of the body that elicit a sexual reaction. This can include the genital location, nipple areas, or anywhere, really-- whatever you're right into.

The clitoris belongs to the vulva, the name for the outside parts of female genitalia. The vagina is the tube connecting the cervix as well as the vulva.

The clitoris and also vaginal canal are thought about components of the vulva as well as internal sex body organs. The clitoris is very sensitive, made up of even more than 8,000 sensory-nerve closings, and is linked with initiating orgasms; 90% of ladies can orgasm by clitoral excitement alone.

WHAT IS THE CLITORIS? AND ALSO, WHERE IS IT?

For women and individuals with vaginas, climaxes most frequently come from the clitoris, located above the genital opening and also urethra.

The clitoris is the primary resource of female sex-related satisfaction.

Right here is a representation of a vulva:

Where is the clitoris? Allow's take a look at the makeup.

The clitoris is not merely the part of your vulva that seems like a little switch.

Many individuals with vaginas-- regardless of perhaps getting and appreciating delighted from penetrative sex-- don't constantly orgasm from sexual intercourse.

Stimulation of the clitoris can be applied straight, inside (through the vagina), and via stimulation of the other parts of the vulva.

Straight excitement to the glans clitoris or clitoral hood is usually needed for the final push to get to climax .

The clitoris is composed of multiple parts:

Unlike the remainder of the clitoris, the glans does not expand or swell throughout the sexual activity, as it does not have erectile (growing) cells.

- The Glans
- the clitoral body
- the paired crura and vestibular bulbs.
- Outside parts of the clitoris

The glans clitoris is the name of the exterior part of the clitoris-- the component that most people call the "clitoris.".

It is about the size of a pea, and also lies above the urethra. It's very sensitive to touch because the glans is the most highly innervated area of the clitoris.

From the body (located before the urethra), the clitoris divides in half to form the combined crura (these are like the "legs" of the clitoris), and vestibular bulbs. These bulbs extend through and also behind the labia, going by the urethra, vaginal canal, and in the direction of the rectum.

Internal parts of the clitoris.

The majority of the clitoris is not commonly visible.

Directly over or in addition to the glans is the clitoral hood, which is developed by the two sides of the attaching labia minora, Clitoral shades can vary in size and also a level of insurance coverage from one person to another.

The light bulbs and crura consist of erectile tissue that swells with blood throughout women sexual arousal. By increasing on either side of the vaginal canal, they raise lubrication in the vaginal area, while raising sexual stimulation and also experience. This development of clitoral tissue can likewise cause stress to be put on the former of the genital canal.

Connected to the glans clitoris is the body of the clitoris. The clitoral body jobs upwards right into your hips, as well as connects using tendons to your pubic bone.

How to stimulate the clitoris

Everyone is different, as well as has various sexual erogenous areas, wishes, and turn-ons. We can not emphasise this sufficient! There are no "one finest means" to promote the clitoris-- you'll need to do some trying out.

That being claimed, below are some suggestions to aid you, and your companion gets off.

1. Establish a state of mind. Remain in a place in which you feel comfortable.

If you are with a companion, setting the mood could include kissing, sexual activity, as well as checking out each other's bodies.

Feel free to obtain comfortable with any various other erogenous areas of your body (like your nipple areas) if you are flying solo. Do not forget your mind-- if you desire as well as aren't feeling especially activated by your imagination, you can likewise obtain your head in the game with some porn or hot literary works.

2. Present on your own to the location near to the clitoris.

Making use of whatever you like: your fingers, your companion's finger's or mouth/tongue, or an additional (tidy) object like a sex toy. You can additionally try utilising a showerhead, vibrator, or even the friction of your underclothing versus something, like a cushion. As soon as you feel comfy with the area around the clitoris as well as prepare, it's time to stimulate the clitoris directly.

3. Starting delicately and softly, touch or stroke the clitoris.

The clitoris is not just a magic button, so merely pressing it (for most individuals) will not immediately create a climax. Don't make-believe to be a DJ either by forcefully scraping it to and fro-- nobody such as that.

4. Take your time.

It's a small area, as well as may appear discouraging at first. "How can I be creative ade uate to stimulate such a little location of skin?" Listen to your body, or your companion, and get comments on what feels excellent.

You might try mild back and forth activities, tiny circular movements, and even a light tap.

Involve the clitoral hood as well-- remember, it additionally has nerve endings as well as the body of the clitoris curves back behind it, before ending up being buried inside your hips. Sign in with yourself or your partner-- does this feel great?

5. You can start to explore pressure, speed, body parts (like tongues if you are with a companion), toys, or vibration.

When most individuals are turned on, they begin to generate arousal liquid, which can aid make promoting the clitoris and also vagina a lot more comfortable.

6. Take into consideration adding some individual lubricating substance to the mix.

We're big followers of lube.

7. You can additionally try promoting the clitoris from the inside, making use of a penis, sex-toy, or fingers.

Not every person will certainly be able to be stimulated or even get to orgasm the very first time, or every time, they have sex or masturbate-- which's alright.

Clitoris research as well as the G-spot

The clitoris-- both its composition and feature-- is a fiercely ⬚uestioned topic. Taboos regarding discussing females' sexuality as well as satisfaction have added to the lack of study in these areas. Yet as taboo are damaged, further research will with any luck supply more ⬚uality in comprehending the clitoris.

The existence or feature of the G-spot is not 100 per cent clear. Some study asserts maybe connected with women ejaculation (likewise called "spraying").

Various other researchers recommend that the G-spot isn't necessarily an actual physical entity, however, preferably the area where the sides of the vestibular light bulbs of the clitoris make contact with the former wall surface of the vagina.

This recommends that a "vaginal orgasm" may still be attached to the clitoris-- each propelled during penetrative genital sexual intercourse or contraction of the pelvic muscles-- can promote the clitoris.

Clitoris size

The exterior part of the clitoris, the glans clitoris, as well as the clitoral hood, can vary significantly from person to person.

At eight weeks of fetal development, the Y chromosome on male DNA will activate the differentiation of the genital cells to become a penis, rather than a clitoris. Many of the parts of the clitoris resemble that of the penis, but vary in shape and also dimension, and also are located in different areas.

Exposure to androgens can cause the clitoris to enlarge during any life phase, including during growth in the womb, throughout childhood years, and also throughout their adult years. When a clitoris dimension is big enough to be considered irregular, this is called clitoromegaly.

The penis as well as the clitoris-- a standard beginning

The penis and also the clitoris are related in structure to one another. They originate from the same developmental tissue.

The only real vital thing is that you appreciate on your own. Do not do it if you aren't having enjoyable.

Is the clitoris a small penis-- or the penis a large clitoris?

Everyone gets to climax differently. Experimenting with self-pleasure or sex settings-- and also having patience-- can assist you in finding out what works best for you.

The vagina, likewise called the "birth canal," is a muscular canal that spans from the cervix to the introitus. It has a typical overall fired up length of about four and also a half inches and also has two parts: First, there are the internal two-thirds -- developed during the first trimester of maternity. Second, there is the external one-third of the vaginal canal. It is created throughout the 2nd trimester of motherhood as well as is usually more sensitive than the inner portion, however drastically much less delicate than the clitoris (Hines, 2001). Only between 10% and also 30% of women attain orgasms by genital stimulation alone (Thompson, 2016). At each end of the vaginal area is the cervix (the reduced part of the womb) and also the introitus (the genital opening to the outside of the body). The vaginal canal serves as a transport system for sperm cells being available in, as well as menstruation fluid and also infants going out. A healthy and balanced vaginal area has a pH degree of concerning four, which is acidic. When the pH level adjustments, often as a result of typical scenarios (e.g., menstruation, making use of tampons, intercourse), it facilitates the recreation of microorganisms that often cause genital smell as well as pain. This potential issue can be fixed with over the counter dental probiotics or vaginal gels to keep normal genital pH levels.

The primary features of the inner sex organs of the female are to shop, transport, as well as keep egg cells (eggs) healthy and balanced; and produce hormones.

These organs include:

(a) the uterus (or womb)-- where human advancement occurs up until birth;

(b) the ovaries-- the glands that house the ova (eggs; concerning two million;) and also create progesterone, estrogen, and even percentages of testosterone;

(c) The fallopian tubes-- where fertilisation is most likely to happen. These tubes enable ovulation (about every 28 days), which is when ova are travelling from the ovaries to the uterus. Menstruation starts if fertilisation does not happen. Menstrual cycle, likewise called a "duration," is the discharge of ova together with the cellular lining of the uterus through the vaginal area, usually taking several days to finish.

MALE ANATOMY

The penis's significant features are initiating orgasm, and also moving semen as well as urine from the body. On standard, a drooping penis is regarding three as well as a fifty per cent inches in size, whereas an erect penis is regarding 5 inches (Veale et al., 2015; Wessells, Lue & McAninch, 1996). If you desire to understand the size of a certain man's erect penis, you'll have actually to see it-- because there are no trustworthy correlations between the length of an upright penis and also

(a) the length of a drooping penis, (b) the measures of other body components-- including feet, hands, lower arms, and also general height-- or (c) race as well as ethnic culture

In addition to the penis, various other male exterior sex body organs have two main functions: producing hormonal agents and sperm cells. The scrotum is the cavity of skin behind as well as below the penis, including the testicles. The testicles (or testes) are the glands that produce testosterone, progesterone, percentages of estrogen, as well as sperm cells.

Many people are usually surprised to discover that males likewise have inner sex organs. The superior capabilities of male interior sex organs happen to be transporting sperm tissues, keeping sperm tissue healthy, and providing semen--the fluid where sperm cells are usually carried. The male's inside sex organs incorporate:

(a) the epididymis, which is a twisted duct that matures, shops, and transports sperm tissues into the vas deferens;

(b) the vas deferens--a muscular tubing that transports mature sperm for the urethra, except in men who have experienced a vasectomy;

(c) The seminal vesicles--glands are offering vitality for sperm skin cells to go. This energy will be through sugar (fructose) also it composes about 75% with the semen. Sperm tissues only create about 1% on the semen;

(d) the prostate gland, which gives additional fluid for the semen that nourishes the sperm tissue; plus the Cowper's glands, which create a substance that lubricates the urethra and neutralises any acidity because of urine;

(e) the urethra--the pipe that provides urine and semen outside the body.

SEX ON THE MIND

Initially glance--or touch with the matter--the clitoris and penis will be the parts of our bodies that appear to bring probably the most pleasure. However, both of these organs pale compared to our central anxious system's convenience of comfort. Extensive parts of the mind and brainstem are usually activated whenever a person experiences to delight, consisting of the insula, temporal cortex, limbic program, nucleus accumbens, basal ganglia, remarkable parietal cortex, dorsolateral prefrontal cortex, and cerebellum. Neuroimaging approaches show these regions of the mind are dynamic when patients contain spontaneous orgasms including no immediate stimulation of your skin so when experimental members self-stimulate erogenous areas. Erogenous zones are sensitive regions of skin which are linked, via the anxious system, towards the somatosensory cortex in mind.

The somatosensory cortex (SC) may be the area of the brain primarily in charge of processing sensitive info from your skin. The more hypersensitive an area of one's skin is undoubtedly (e.g., your mouth), the bigger the corresponding section of the SC will undoubtedly be; the less susceptible an area of one's skin can be (e.g., your trunk), small the relevant section of the SC will undoubtedly be. Whenever a sensitive part of a person's body is touched, it is commonly interpreted by the mind in another of 3 ways: "That tickles!" "That hurts!" or, "That...you must do again!" Consequently, the more delicate areas of our anatomies have greater possible to evoke enjoyment. A report by Nummenmaa and his fellow workers (2016) used a distinctive method to try this hypothesis. The Nummenmaa analysis team exhibited experimental participants pictures of similar- and opposite-sex body. They then enquired the individuals to colour the parts of your body that, when handled, they or associates of the contrary sex would feel as sexually arousing while masturbating or possessing sex with somebody. Nummenmaa identified the predicted "hotspot" erogenous areas around the external sex organs, chests, and anus, but additionally reported regions of your skin beyond these hotspots: "[T]actile stimulation of pretty much all bodily locations cause sexual arousal...." Furthermore, he concluded, "[H]aving sex with somebody..."--beyond the hotspots--"...demonstrates the part of touching inside the maintenance of...couple bonds."

SEXUAL REACTION CYCLE

The sexual reaction cycle involves the stages of need, arousal, orgasm and □uality. Each step of this cycle is referred to.

WHAT'S THE SEXUAL REACTION CYCLE?

The sexual reaction cycle identifies the series of actual and emotional improvements that happen as an individual gets to be sexually aroused and participates in sexually rousing activities, incorporating intercourse and masturbation. Focusing on how your system responds during each stage from the cycle can boost your romantic relationship and assist you to pinpoint the reason for sexual dysfunction. It isn't the only style of a sexual reply cycle. Nonetheless, it is the better-known one.

WHICH ARE THE PHASES OF THIS SEXUAL REACTION CYCLE?

The sexual reaction cycle provides four stages: need (sex drive), arousal (enthusiasm), orgasm and image resolution. Men and women experience these stages, even though timing usually differs. For example, it is improbable that both lovers will get to orgasm at precisely the same time. Furthermore, the depth of the reply and enough time expended in each stage varies from individual to individual. Many women won't feel the sexual phases in this particular order. A few of these stages could be absent during some sexual encounters, or away from a collection in others. A desire to have intimacy might be a determination for sexual action in some persons. Understanding these variances may help associates better have an understanding of one another's systems and replies, and improve the sexual experience.

Several physiologic improvements might occur during different periods of sexual action. Individuals may encounter some, all, or nothing of these alterations.

Period 1: Desire

General characteristics of the phase, that may last from the few minutes to many hours, are the following:

Muscle tension boosts.

Heart rate quickens, and respiration is accelerated.

The skin could become flushed (blotches of inflammation look on the upper body and rear).

Nipples become solidified or erect.

Blood flow towards the genitals increases, leading to swelling of the girl clitoris and labia minora (interior lip area), and erection on the man's penis.

Vaginal lubrication starts.

The woman's boobies become fuller along with the vaginal walls commence swelling.

The man's testicles swell, his scrotum tightens, and he commences secreting a lubricating liquid

Period 2: Arousal

General characteristics of the phase, which reaches the brink of orgasm, are the following:

The changes started in stage 1 are usually intensified.

The vagina is continuously on the swell from raised blood flow, along with the vaginal walls, convert a dark crimson.

The girl clitoris becomes remarkably sensitive (could even be painful to the touch) and retracts beneath the clitoral hood to avoid direct stimulation from the penis.

The man's testicles will be withdrawn up into the scrotum.

Breathing, heart rate and blood circulation pressure continue to enhance.

Muscle spasms can start in your toes, face and palms.

The tension inside the muscles increases.

Stage 3: Orgasm

This phase may be the climax from the sexual response routine. It's the shortest in the aspects and commonly lasts just a few seconds. General features of this period include them here:

Involuntary muscles contractions begin.

Blood pressure, heart rate and breathing are at their highest costs, with an instant intake of air.

Muscles in your toes spasm.

There's a sudden, forceful launch of sexual anxiety.

In ladies, the muscles on the vagina deal. The uterus as well as undergoes rhythmic contractions.

In guys, rhythmic contractions on the muscles at the bottom on the penis bring about the ejaculations of semen.

A rash or "sex flush" can happen over the system.

Period 4: Resolution

During this period, the body slowly and gradually profits to its ordinary level of performing and swelled, and erect areas of the body go back to their previous measurement and colouring. This phase is usually marked by way of a general perception of well-being and, generally, fatigue. Some ladies can handle a rapid go back to the orgasm stage with further intimate stimulation and could experience several orgasms. Men require a recovery period after orgasm, referred to as a refractory period, during which they can not reach orgasm once again. The length of the refractory time varies among adult males and modifications with age.

INDIVIDUAL SEXUAL BEHAVIOR

Human sex, human sexual exercise or human erotic behavior may be the way humans knowledge and communicate their sexuality. Persons engaged in several sexual acts, which range from activities done by itself (e.g., masturbation) to works with someone else (e.g., sexual activity, non-penetrative sex, dental gender, etc.) in differing patterns of consistency, for a multitude of reasons. Sex usually results in erotic arousal and physiological adjustments in the aroused particular person. Some of that happen to be pronounced while some are more understated. Sexual activity could also include doing and activities which can be designed to arouse the erotic fascination of another or improve the sex life of another, such for example strategies to discover or attract lovers (courtship and screen behavior), or private interactions between folks (for instance, foreplay or BDSM). Sex may follow intimate arousal.

Human sex features sociological, cognitive, psychological, behavioral and natural aspects; included in these are personal bonding, discussing emotions along with the physiology with the reproductive system, libido, sexual activity, and sexual behavior in every its forms.

In a few cultures, sex is considered satisfactory only within matrimony, while premarital and extramarital making love happen to be taboo. Some intimate activities are unlawful either universally or in a few international locations or subnational jurisdictions, although some are considered unlike the norms of selected societies or cultures

Human sex, any activity--solitary, between two individuals, or in a group--that induces intimate arousal. You can find two main determinants of individual sex: the inherited erotic response patterns which have evolved as a way of ensuring duplication and which are an integral part of each individual's hereditary inheritance, and the amount of restraint or other styles of the effect exerted on people by society inside the expression of these sexualities. The target here is to spell it out and make clear both packages of variables and their connections.

It ought to be observed that taboos in American culture as well as the immaturity of this social sciences for an extended period impeded research relating to human sex, in order that by the first 20th century technological knowledge was mostly restricted to particular case histories that were studied by many of these European freelance writers as Sigmund Freud, Havelock Ellis, and Richard, Freiherr (baron) von Krafft-Ebing. From the 1920s, even so, the foundations have been laid for the even more extensive statistical research that were performed before World Battle II in America. Of both major companies for sex research, one, the Institut f? R Sexualwissenschaft in Berlin (established in 1897), was initially destroyed by Nazis in 1933. Another, the Institute for Love-making Research (in the future renamed Kinsey Institute for Exploration in Sex, Sex, and Duplication), started in 1938 from the North American sexologist Alfred Charles Kinsey at Indiana University or college in Bloomington, undertook the analysis of human sexuality. Much of the next discourse rests on the studies of this Institute for Intimacy Study, which constitute probably the most comprehensive data out there. The only additional country that complete data can be found in Sweden.

FORMS OF ACTIVITY

Human sex may conveniently turn out to be classified based on the number and intercourse of the members. There's solitary activity affecting only one person, and there's sociosexual activity concerning several people. Sociosexual exercise a perfect for heterosexual practice (males with feminine) and homosexual tasks (man with female or male with a girl). If three or even more individuals are engaged, it is possible to possess heterosexual and homosexual tasks simultaneously.

Both in solitary and sociosexual exercise, there could be activities that are sufficiently different to warrant the content label abnormal activity. The word deviant shouldn't be used as being a moral judgment but merely as indicating that like the action isn't every day in a specific society. Since human being societies differ within their sexual practices, what's deviant in a single community could be standard in another Sexuality. It is a pretty sexy phrase in itself, and its meaning has developed to mean various things as time passes. Sexuality is an assortment of our sexual qualities, and it's, in fact, an essential part of how exactly we convey ourselves as humans. It's not merely just the act of experiencing sex, but it is also part of how exactly we relate with ourselves, among others, and exhibit the physical, mental, and maybe possibly spiritual elements of our personalities.

Although advertising and cultural effects perform their darndest to steer our perceptions of how sexuality "should" come to be expressed, these illustrations only represent a little section of people's thoughts and steps around sexuality. Most of whatever we see on the net, TV, or video displays perpetuates a slim and unrealistic representation of sexuality and romantic relationships. Even more, the reason to only discuss it and keep carefully the dialogue rooted in what's right, wouldn't you point out?.

ASEXUALITY-UNDERSTANDING MEN'S SEXUAL AND EMOTIONAL NEEDS

These are intimate ideas and behaviors at the average person level.

Guy masturbation frequencies fluctuate significantly, indicating not just a selection in responsiveness but additionally the different informed choices men generate over the way they take pleasure in their 'arousal routine' from erection to ejaculations.

Sex is mental for men since it links them with women, friends and family, and society. Man mammals tend to be solitary animals. They connect to other males to be able to defend territory sufficient reason for females to be ready to mate. Men usually do not share their views and feelings mainly because easily as women carry out. So we declare that women will be psychological and men aren't. Yet some people use hostility (an emotional behavior) expressing anger, stress, and fear.

When confronting an enemy, it is helpful if we can don't be paralyzed with anxiety or bursting into tears. We have to have the ability to channel any rage and apprehension we might feel into extreme action. Conse□uently, aggression is known as a strength since it is a resource if we have been facing an actual physical threat. Tears, alternatively, are usually an indicator of weakness. The associated emotional state could be debilitating. You'll find nothing wrong with possessing a great cry so long as you are not attempting to save the planet (which women aren't designed to perform). Crying can be a proven way of venting our feelings.

A man can make an improved aggressor and defender because his testosterone ranges help him reply better in ruthless circumstances. Testosterone urges men to take chances (even more than others clearly!). General men choose higher stakes than women are prepared to engage in for. Despite our contemporary and sophisticated weaponry, films nevertheless depict stars in arm-to-arm fight or wrestling. A hands-on fist battle expresses the feelings of a far more personal type of combat. Men battle (and play sports activity) to help significantly dissipate the tensions developed by their intercourse and individual drives.

Men could be distracted by way of a beautiful woman. Nonetheless, it is a distraction. They're much more worried about the risk of another man. Males may demand that sex is key to their welfare, but their territorial intuition comes very first. Some put jobs before marriage while others price the comradeship and adrenaline hurry of a wearing event on the sexual prospect. Despite men's libido, it is almost always women who produce relationships work.

Males fight one another for breeding protection under the law, and they reduce the chance to mate should they cannot beat competitors. Females partner with guys who win privileges over information (to sustain a family group) and who can shield them from additional males. In individuals terms, we discover that women incline to gravitate towards men who can provide defence and way of living through cash flow or status

SEXUAL BEHAVIOR OUTSIDE AND INSIDE THE BEDROOM

Focus on how your sexual model and behavior tends to make your partner experience themselves and the partnership because your intimate style could be hurting your human relationships..

1. The Sexual Visitors Cop

The results of the G-spot misconception is not exclusively because of men's ignorance of the feminine anatomy involved with orgasm. Women of all ages who never learn to stimulate themselves as well choose explanations for the female orgasm that depend on male libido rather than independently motivation to accomplish orgasm.

A defining facet of women's sexuality is undoubtedly their willingness to pay for their insufficient responsiveness by participating in behaviors which are possibly consciously or subconsciously inspired. Although she never comes with an orgasm, a female behaves sexually by participating in intercourse.

Women are, in a natural way, cooperative presented their reliance on others. So women locate ways of satisfying men and accommodating their wants.

Women suppose a passive position in sex, letting men supply not merely the stimulation but additionally the enthusiasm they keep company with lovemaking. Men activate the anatomy (chests and vagina) that helps to make use of their arousal. But it has nothing in connection with how a girl achieves her very own orgasm.

A woman does not have any have to orgasm, which has a lover, but a guy might need reassurance that she appreciates his functionality and his erotic admiration.

To increase male orgasm, a skilled woman plays alongside male's fantasies by exaggerating her arousal and faking an orgasm. This 'responsiveness' to be a lover has nothing in connection with her very own orgasmic ability.

Women's accomplishments with faking could very well be the significant hoax ever.

Many people happen to be outraged from the recommendation that anyone might misrepresent women's sexuality or exaggerate feminine responsiveness. But in the areas of adult living, we explain to untruths (or flex the reality) regularly.

Humans beings tend to be more worried about impressing or influencing others than with any basic principle as prosaic as 'the reality.' When our motives happen to be well-intentioned (to show tact or diplomacy) like behavior is known as to become compassionate or politically astute instead of deceitful.

Outside the master bedroom: The Intimate Traffic Cop is precisely what we would contact a typical handle freak.

They often feel that these were placed on this globe to "put others within their location" and think obligated to inform others what's 'proper' and what's "wrong." They have a propensity to believe their ideas, their families, associations or careers are usually what everyone should emulate and don't think twice flaunting them in public areas for everybody to copy. They are generally critical and strenuous, always giving re□uests and creating rules. They could be extremely picky, impatient, and judgmental, regularly giving advice, fixing, or "mothering" others.

Inside the room: When you have sex having a Sexual Site visitors Cop, you'll get so many instructions and instructions on which he/she wants and doesn't prefer. They will inform you the way you should sense and respond, plus they may show you how they need you to take action to them and have you to carry out precisely the approach they take effect. You generate one "wrong" shift, and he/she stops and won't continue. The most detrimental part is that we now have so many directions that you won't ever seem to bear in mind what they enjoy or can't stand. You are feeling pressured, manipulated and inadequate each time.

2. The Sexual Beast

Outside the bedroom: The Erotic Beast usually speaks loudly - and unclean. They are the type of people who are everywhere and are possibly disillusioned that others enjoy them or typically do not care if they're liked or not necessarily. They have a powerful have to dominate others also to be in the cost of things. They could appear very handled but happen to be cynical and temperamental, and □uickly explode into fury when their specialist or intelligence is undoubtedly challenged. They could be incredibly vindictive and manipulative. They aren't angry at the contrary sex. It's that they mistake aggression and chaos with enthusiasm and spontaneity.

Inside the room: When you have sex using a Sexual Beast, you aren't sure whether you're being liked or devoured. His/her panting, getting, slapping, scratching, biting, driving, tugging, and bestial sounds or "dirty discuss" minimizes the sex action to its pretty basic crude levels. You are kept frightened, distrustful, unsatisfied and irritated but not sure why.

3. The Sexual Martyr

Outside the master bedroom: The Sexual Martyr resides with a sufferer mentality. They're always revealing to "poor me" reviews, blaming others for precisely what has happened in their minds. They don't consider they're lovable or worth it and discover it difficult expressing their re□uirements or require what they need. They've never really had satisfying encounters and feel applied and rooked regularly.

Inside the room: When you have sex having an Intimate Martyr, you experience that "something" indefinitely not right, but on the other hand, much you talk to, he/she won't tell. The only path they make an effort to inform you what is occurring is once you play the role of intimate, their primary reaction would be to move away just a little or rest right now there motionless. You type of strat to get resentful as you can't go through his/her mind, and you also come to feel guilty for not really having the ability to figure out what's really occurring.

4. The Sexual Procrastinator

Outside the room: The Sexual Procrastinator avoids undertaking things he/she must do or cope with and hates getting told how to proceed. They re□uire advice, make aims and guarantees, but never really get to have them out. They're usually very logical and realistic and have themselves seriously. They could be pretty talkative, impressionable, compassionate and heated but feel uneasy about approaching other people and fre□uently avoid these circumstances.

Inside the bedroom: Should anyone ever get to have sexual intercourse with an Erotic Procrastinator consider yourself probably one of the most patient people on the planet because, by enough time you can actually have intimacy with this personality, you'll have read all sorts of logical explanations concerning how the ambience, timing, and the area is simply not right. But perhaps during sex, they'll find little complications to interrupt or power you to quit. You are remaining feeling controlled, ignored, desperate and irritated.

5. The Sexual Glutton

Outside the master bedroom: The Intimate Glutton is a professional at making the most of him/herself. Intimate Gluttons have a very low tolerance to soreness or suffering and so are often susceptible to addictive behaviors. They often seek out sex toys to try out with, so when they find a thing that gives them satisfaction, food, alcohol, medicines, etc. they obtain completely shed in discomfort oblivious of individuals and everything around them.

Inside the room: When you have sex using a Sexual Glutton, you obtain the feeling you're just a plaything for their delight. If you make an effort to change what you are doing to provide them enjoyment, they motion for you to keep going, forking over no consideration whatsoever in your feelings. When you experience "high and dried," he/she is at his/her pleasure globe. You are kept feeling overlooked, unimportant, unloved and irritated at used

6. The Sexual Performer

Outside the room: The Intimate Performer is usually wildly thinking about everything. Everything and many people are always fantastic, great, amazing, fabulous, excellent, brilliant, etc. Once you meet this identity, you are practically sure he/she may be the most passionate particular person you've ever found, yet you obtain a feeling that there surely is something nearly proper about his/her love - you're perhaps right. Intimate Performers are individuals who need to get near others but are usually so restless about intimacy they often frighten others away.

Inside the master bedroom: When you have sex which has a Sexual Performer, you obtain the feeling they're gaining an express; they create a lot of sounds, and they'll do that and do this, fre□uently changing placements and letting you know again and again how fabulous it is. They'll even demand sex is way better before a mirror since they want to check out themselves carry out. Their "pleasure" looks so exaggerated that you will be not sure whether it's gender or their overall performance that they enjoy so much. You're left feeling employed, mistrustful, and also resentful.

7. The Erotic Idealist

Outside the master bedroom: The Erotic Idealist is very sensitive, powerful, and incredibly intelligent. They're usually religious and philosophical, and so are passionate concerning the protection of the surroundings, cruelty against wildlife, and universe poverty. They desperately wish fairness and goodness for everybody and in everything because their previous experiences have already been the opposite. They might be kids of divorced or psychologically isolated and dissociated moms, and dads were used or resided with parents who have been kept busy operating. Because they have already been abandoned over and over, they might be deluded that their function, relationships, and lifetime are perfect and so are afraid to check out life honestly since they worry that their constructive prospect may collapse.

ADDICTIVE EROTIC BEHAVIOR

The term addiction originates from the Latin 'advertising dictum' - towards the dictator.

Sex Addiction is a relatively newly recognized phenomenon. Lots of people find it hard to believe that intercourse itself is an addiction.

But generally, any addiction isn't well understood. The essential element of a dependency is undoubtedly a loss of handle over the charge or occurrence of the experience, coupled with improving damaging life repercussions.

So sex exercise can quite definitely belong to this category for many individuals. To lose management of a task is usually to be powerless on the ability to handle it.

The term 'powerless' conjures up various ideas. It necessarily implies that whatever power must make healthy options in our mental and intimate behavior didn't reside within us. It ends up with enslavement to gender and takes pleasure in, manifested as a psychological dependency and compulsive, friendly expression.

It issues little whether our styles happen to be rampant promiscuity or high emotional dependency using one particular person, or some mix of these — lack of control results in a feeling of genuine desperation. To keep to call home in this problem brings one to the terror of burning off your sanity as well as the realization a meaningful existence and emotional stableness will be eternally from the reach. This potential customer is usually terrifying and turns with time to a whole descent into depressive disorder and demoralization.

Loss of handle has become a recognized fact. All attempts to control the addiction or no cost ourselves, as a result, are futile, resulting in further more demoralization and despair.

Symptoms of love-making and take pleasure in addiction:

- Compulsive Masturbation

- Loss of an initial relationship such for example marriage because of external sex.

- Spending money it is possible to ill find the money for on prostitutes.

- Obsessive courting through online dating services.

- Engaging in erotic harassment.

- Unable to keep a connection despite repeated endeavours to take action.

- Obsessively yearning for your relationship but incapable or reluctant to initiate contact with a potential mate.

- Obsessively seeing porn, generally to the detriment of different more responsible exercise.

- Engaging in pc and phone intimacy.

- Indulging in unprotected sex despite the apparent risks to your wellbeing and wellbeing.

- Deriving little if any satisfaction from your sex and creating no emotional relationship with your love-making partners.

The above record is not designed to turn out to be exhaustive as each individual must comprehend their unique designs of addiction.

Experience implies that the best method of freeing oneself from addiction would be to unconditionally accept that you will be completely powerless to regulate or handle the behavior.

FORMS OF SEX OBSESSION "DON'T PERCEIVE IT AS LOVE"

The distinction between 10 forms of addictive sexual behavior plus the intimacy you'll experience using what he phone calls "genuine like."

Opinions in what constitutes problematic erotic behavior change among specialists and the general public. A few of these behaviors, such for example fantasy sex, arise in healthy intimate relationships, while some, such for instance exploitative sex, are usually highly problematic in virtually any context.

FANTASY SEX

Fantasy sex is a preoccupying obsession with intimate fantasy, as opposed to the reality of reputable sexual feelings, friendly behavior, and close relationships. It could avoid you from building genuine loving thoughts based on taking others the direction they are.

SEDUCTIVE PURPOSE SEX

Seductive sex targets lovely, persuading, or manipulating others into intimate contact. You take care of your prospective spouse as being a "con□uest" or perhaps a challenge to create yourself feel better.

ANONYMOUS SEX

Anonymous sex is certainly sex with stranger like one night appears you discover on Tinder. Private sex assists the addict to to steer clear of developing genuine caring feelings.

SPENDING MONEY ON SEX

Paying for making love also inhibits gengenuine connection, due to the implied business layout. The individual you pay wants financial gain, not just a loving relationship.

TRADING SEX

The other area on the paying-for-sex transaction receives money or merchandise for intimacy or using love-making as a small business. Sex results in being a commodity, instead of personal experience, as well as the emotional interconnection, diminishes.

VOYEURISTIC SEX

Voyeuristic sex targets watching others take part in sexual activity. You obtain sexually aroused by considering pornography from:

• Guides and magazines

• The personal computer and films

• Peep-shows

• Secretly observing other folks, just like a peeping Tom

• Going to intimacy clubs to view in person

Excessive masturbation, possibly to the stage of injury, is certainly typical for voyeurs. They take part in solitary activities, instead of connecting with someone else, guaranteeing intimacy and like aren't an option.

EXHIBITIONISTIC SEX

Exhibitionist sex consists of flashing "forbidden" areas of the body in public, frequently while wearing outfits made to expose. Other styles of exhibitionist gender contain posing for pornographic images and sex, where others can easily see.

Exhibitionism can override real loving connections as the excitement originates from the reaction, definitely not from the erotic relationship with your partner.

INTRUSIVE SEX

Intrusive sex requires coming in contact with others without authorisation. It may entail abusing your situation of electric power or authority, as the function of priest, supervisor, or trainer, to exploit others sexually.

Intrusive sex can be inherently exploitative, rendering it impossible to create the foundationto having confidence in or love. Subjects may experience emotions of loyalty into the perpetrator.

PAIN EXCHANGE

The presenting or obtaining of pain also called sadomasochism or S&M, is a sexually addictive behavior where the consenting members associate discomfort with sexual joy.

Much like intrusive sex, sufferers may understand their emotions towards their torturer as adoring.

EXPLOITATIVE SEX

Rape and paedophilia are usually forms of exploitative intimacy. Because one individual violates the human being's rights of another, there is absolutely no possibility for authentic like or intimacy

While in the bedroom: during sex having a Sexual desire or anticipation to enjoy it not necessarily once but twice: first once you hear the fantastic and many advantages of making love and once more after once you listen to a recounting from the just concluded enchanting working experience. He/she will let you know how sex to you is way much better than all of the ones he/she's obtained all his/her daily life and also just what a great lover you're. You're pushed to implement to similar or extra criteria, simply to proceed. But their "excellent" planet leaves you experiencing inade☐uate, not adored by yourself and also mistrustful of these claims.

THE EROTIC PLEASER

Outside the room: The Intimate Pleaser usually is sweet, cheerful, passionate and great to everyone. They will incline to confuse like with pity, and also a propensity to "love" men and women they can pity and recovery. They are excessively influenced by the agreement of members of these family, spouse, close friends, colleagues and also strangers. They'll head to any measures and overboard to make sure you and when they certainly they will endure there silently using a "so?" seem on their encounter. They can come to be manipulated because Erotic Pleasers have trouble expressing "no' to demands inside and outside of the bedroom.

Inside the master bedroom: When you have sex which has a Sexual Pleaser, you'll feel fantastic - initially - since they come across because of thesuperpartner. They re□uest "Can you such as this or Feel I satisfying you?" They go directly to the measures of apologising if you say you didn't like that. After a few years, you start becoming selfish and guilty. You experience their desperation and have to please and think obligated to him/her but at precisely the same time feel governed by their neediness.

THE SEXUAL CORPSE

Outside the room: The Intimate Corpse can be a pro at repressing his/her thoughts. They appear great, calm and accumulated externally but profound inside they're anxious, apprehensive, and fearful. Numerous have suffered plenty of hurt, pain, disappointment and have ended up abused as kids or by their erotic partners. They often find it hard to trust others also to self-disclose. They don't easily forgive rather than forget. Even though they openly don't point out it, you obtain the feeling speaking with them they are so irritated at the contrary sex.

Inside the room: When you have sex which has an Erotic Corpse, their notion of sex is undoubtedly you enjoying "sex psychic". They by no means show feelings or claim a term before, during or after gender. It is your decision to reckon how they're feeling or should they like sex together with you. It is your choice to determine what they need - or should they even as if you. If you inquire further if they including something the very best they can produce is 'It's fine". You're left inadequate, aggravated and even upset at them.

THE SEXUAL TEASE

Outside the master bedroom: The Erotic Tease may be the kind of male or female who talks about your lover and can make them wish these were single. They simply love to promote how "super-sexy" they - they outfit and stroll the portion. Their whole notion of life will be superficiality - apparel, status etc., and also have a behavior of name-dropping or talking about their links to famous, abundant and powerful men and women. They are incredibly competitive with associates of precisely the same sex and so are usually pretty jealous and possessive folks. The Erotic Tease also offers problems checking and producing commitments to some other person.

Inside the room: Your investment master bedroom - an Erotic Tease occurs □uite active and aggressive, switching you on and travelling you mad with his/her work. But when there's a possibility that making love might happen, the sexy, warm and wild photograph disappears. They begin providing excuses or locate something else to accomplish - to tease you even more. And if you genuinely manage to have sexual intercourse with this personality - you'll be very upset. An Intimate Tease is fired up by the thought of being outrageous and sexy; however, not by the specific act of love-making itself.

Thus:

I believe that there surely is no "right" or "wrong" method of making love. Making love is "fine" when it creates both of one's feel great about yourselves and concerning the relationship which is 'poor" when it finds you miserable and increases your negative emotions about yourself, your lover or about connections. Fortunately that there surely is something it is possible always to carry out to end up being the lover you're capable of staying (detailed on my web page are a number of the things it is possible to perform immediately). The Super Partner is at everyone folks. The item you need first of all is profound insights into the uni□ue, innovative and ultimately mystical being you're. Second, you will need an intuitive knowledge of the elaborate dynamics of man-woman energies. Studying specific techni□ues isn't enough; you should know the interplay between your sexes that's enough to evoke a profound link and smouldering enthusiasm.

SEXUAL HEALTH

Sexual health is undoubtedly influenced by way of a great many aspects ranging from behavior, attitudes, and fitness, to natural and genetic variables. It encompasses the issues of HIV, unintended pregnancy and abortion, infertility and erotic dysfunction. Sexual health and fitness may also be influenced by psychological health, severe and chronic health problems, and violence.

It also entails the individual, relatives, community, health technique level lawful and regulatory conditions where the erotic rights of most folks are upheld.

Suggestions and norms about sexuality and overall health come from some sources including societal custom, science, medication, religious opinion, and personal encounters. Because of this, no one meaning of sexual wellbeing will probably adequately stand for this diversity, mainly when professional ideas on sexuality and erotic health are made by training and societal position which, are often affected with the individual's way of life, socio-economic status, faith, etc.

Because the text "health" and "healthy" tend to be from the field of drugs, they have a medical-related connotation and expert. Because of this, the word "sexual well being" could be misused expressing authorisation or disapproval of certain behaviors or men and women under what might seem to get "medical truth". This is why some love-making teachers and therapists are usually fearful of marketing thought of sexual wellbeing (immediately, by determining it, or indirectly, by acquiring suggestions) through knowledge.

Also, it's worthwhile to remember that definitions of erotic health can transform and should certainly not be studied as rigid guidelines of conduct.

The World Health Organisation says.

"Sexual health is definitely...the integration of this physical, mental, intellectual and societal aspects of intimate being, with techni□ues that are favourably enriching which enhance personality, interaction and like."

"...a capacity to take pleasure from and control erotic and reproductive behavior relative to a sociable and personalised ethic."

"...freedom from concern, shame, guilt, phoney beliefs along with other psychological elements inhibiting intimate response and impairing erotic relationships."

"...freedom from organic and natural disorders, illnesses and deficiencies that hinder intimate and reproductive features."

Good sexual overall health means making sure you have the data, skills and capability to make informed erotic choices and operating responsibly to safeguard your wellbeing and the fitness of others.

PREGNANCY

Among the potential outcomes of this SRC is certainly pregnancy--the time a lady carries a individual within her uterus. So how exactly does this happen?

The process starts during genital intercourse once the males ejaculate, or produces semen. Each ejaculate consists of about 300 million sperm skin cells. These sperm compete to create their way throughout the cervix and into the uterus. Conception generally occurs inside a fallopian tube whenever a single sperm mobile comes into connection with an ovum (egg). The sperm holds either an X- or Y-chromosome to fertilise the ovum--which, itself, typically bears an X-chromosome. These chromosomes, in conjunction with one another, happen to be what determines someone's sex. The mix of two X chromosomes generates a lady zygote (fertilised ovum). The combination of an X and Con chromosome creates a males zygote. XX- or XY-chromosomes shape your 23rd group of chromosomes (virtually all humans have a complete of 46 chromosomes) generally known as your chromosomal making love or genetic gender.

Interestingly, at the very least one Atlanta divorce attorneys 1,000 conceptions result a variant of chromosomal intimacy beyond the typical XX or XY packages. A few of these variations incorporate, XXX, XXY, XYY, or perhaps a solitary X (Dreger, 1998). In some instances, people could have unusual physical features, such as staying taller than usual, having a thick neck, or becoming sterile (struggling to reproduce); however, in many cases, they haven't any cognitive, bodily, or sexual problems (Wisniewski et al., 2000). Practically 15 from every 1,000 births are usually several births (twins, triplets, □uadruplets, etc.). These may appear in several techni□ues. Dizygotic (fraternal) births will be the result of a lady releasing several ova which several is fertilized by sperm. Because sperm take either X or Con chromosomes, fraternal births could be any mix of sexes (e.g., two women or a guy and a woman). They produce together within the uterus and so are usually born within a few minutes of 1 another. Monozygotic (e□uivalent) births derive from a particular situation when a fertilised ovum splits into several identical embryos plus they develop simultaneously. Equivalent twins are, subse□uently, the same love-making.

Hrs after conception, the zygote starts dividing into extra cells. After that, it starts travelling along with the fallopian tubing until it gets into the uterus as the blastocyst. The blastocyst implants itself in the wall on the cervix to turn into an embryo. Nevertheless, the proportion of prosperous implantations remains to be a mystery. Scientists believe the failure rate to get up to 60%. Failed blastocysts happen to be eradicated during menstruation, generally without the women ever being aware of conception occurred.

Mothers are expectant for three trimesters, a name that begins making use of their last menstrual time and stops about 40 2 or 3 weeks afterwards; each trimester can be 13 weeks. Through the first trimester, a lot of the body parts of this embryo are developed, although at this time they are certainly not in precisely the same proportions because they will undoubtedly be at birth. The mind and head, for instance, account for about 50 % of your body at this time. During the 5th and sixth 2 or 3 weeks of gestation, the primitive gonads are usually formed. They gradually become ovaries or testes. Before the seventh full week, the creating embryo gets the potential of experiencing either men (Wolffian ducts) or feminine (Mullerian ducts) inner sex organs, no matter chromosomal sex. There's an innate trend for several embryos to possess female internal intimacy organs, unless there's the current presence of the SRY gene, on the Y-chromosome. The SRY gene reasons XY-embryos to build up testes (dividing skin cells through the medulla). The testes emit testosterone which stimulates the introduction of male internal intercourse organs--the Wolffian ducts changing into the epididymis, seminal vesicles, and vas deferens. The testes, in addition, give off a Mullerian inhibiting chemical, a hormone that triggers the Mullerian ducts to atrophy. In case the SRY gene isn't found or active--typical for chromosomal ladies (XX)--then XX-embryos develop ovaries (dividing tissue through the cortex) plus the Mullerian ducts change into female interior sex organs, like the fallopian pipes, uterus, cervix, and interior two-thirds from the vagina (Carlson, 1986). Without a burst of testosterone through the testes, the Wolffian ducts by natural means deteriorate.

During the next trimester, pregnant ladies can feel motion within their wombs. That is referred to as quickening. In the uterus, the embryo advances beautiful hair around its body system (named lanugo) in addition to eyelashes and eyebrows. Vital organs, like the pancreas and liver organ, begin fully operating. By 20th few days of gestation, the outside sex organs happen to be fully formed, which explains why "sex conviction" applying ultrasound during this period is more exact than in the initial trimester. Development of male outside sex body organs (e.g., the penis and scrotum) depends upon high degrees of testosterone, whereas feminine external sex body organs (e.g., the outside third on the vagina as well as the clitoris) web form without hormonal effects. Degrees of sex hormones, such for example estrogen, testosterone, and progesterone, start affecting the mind in this trimester, impacting long term emotions, habits, and thoughts linked to gender identification and erotic orientation (Swaab, 2004). It is critical to recognize that the connections of chromosomal gender, gonadal sex, gender hormones, internal intercourse organs, external intercourse organs, and head differentiation in this developmental stage happen to be too intricate to readily comply with the familiar types of sex, sex, and intimate orientation historically applied to describe persons.

Toward the finish of the next trimester--at concerning the 26th week--is age viability, when success outside the uterus includes a probability of a lot more than 90%. Oddly enough, technological improvements and adjustments in-hospital treatment have affected age viability in a way that feasibility can be done earlier in gestation.

During the 3rd trimester, there's a rapid expansion in mind and fast putting on weight. Typically, by 36th 7 days, the fetus commences descending head-first into the uterine cavity. Planning for birth isn't the only actions exhibited in this previous trimester. Erectile replies in males fetuses occur during this time; and Giorgi and Siccardi (1996) noted ultrasonographic observations of your fetus doing self-exploration of her exterior sex organs. Just about all babies are blessed vaginally (throughout the vagina), though in America one-third are usually by Cesarean segment . A newborn's well being is initially dependant on his/her excess fat (usually varying between 2,500 and 4,000 grams)--though labour and birth weight significantly is different between ethnicities.

BIRTH CONTROL

Contraception, or contraceptive, reduces the likelihood of pregnancy caused by sexual intercourse. There are many forms of contraceptive, integrating: hormonal, hurdle, or all-natural. As proven in Stand 1, the potency of the different types of birth control amounts commonly, from 68% to 99.9%

Hormonal types of birth control let go artificial estrogen or progestin, which stops ovulation and thickens cervical mucus, rendering it problematic for sperm to attain ova (sexandu.ca/contraception). There are several methods to introduce these human hormones into the human body, integrating: implantable rods, contraceptive pills, shots, transdermal patches, IUDs, and genital rings. For instance, the vaginal diamond ring is 92% successful, easily placed into and removed from the vagina by an individual, and made up of thin plastic formulated with a variety of hormones which are released at that time it is inside the vagina--usually around three weeks.

Barrier types of birth control stop sperm from getting into the uterus by developing a physical hurdle or chemical hurdle toxic to sperm. There are many barrier procedures, adding: vasectomies, tubal ligations, males and feminine condoms, spermicides, diaphragms, and cervical hats. Typically the most prevalent barrier method may be the condom, that is 79-85% efficient. The male's condom is positioned on the penis, whereas the feminine condom is donned in the vagina and suits around the cervix. Condoms avoid fluids from staying exchanged and decrease skin-to-skin contact. Because of this, condoms may also be used to lessen the chance of some sexually sent infections (STIs). Even so, you should note that males and feminine condoms, or two males condoms, shouldn't be worn all together during penetration; the friction between many condoms produces microscopic tears, making them inade□uate.

Natural types of birth control depend on an understanding of the menstrual period and knowing of your body. They are the Fertility Awareness Approach (FAM), lactational amenorrhea techni□ue, and withdrawal. For instance, the FAM is approximately 75% helpful and re□uires checking the menstrual period, and avoiding sexual activity or using other styles of contraceptive through the female's fertile windowpane. About 30% of ladies' productive windows-- the time when a girl is most probably to conceive--are between times ten and seventeen of this menstrual period (Wilcox, Dunson & Baird, 2000). The rest of the 70% of girls experience abnormal and not as much predictable fertile house windows, reducing the efficiency on the FAM.

Other styles of contraceptive that do unfit into the higher than categories incorporate: disaster contraceptive products, the copper IUD, and abstinence. Crisis contraceptive capsules (e.g., System B) delay the discharge of ovum if obtained ahead of ovulation. Disaster contraception is a form of contraceptive typically utilised after unsafe sex, condom mishaps, or erotic assault. The very best kind of disaster contraception may be the copper IUD. A medical expert inserts the IUD with the opening with the cervix and into the uterus. It is a lot more than 99% effective and could be left inside the womb for over a decade. It varies from usual IUDs since it can be hormone-free and makes use of copper ions to generate an inhospitable atmosphere for sperm, hence significantly reducing the probability of fertilisation. Moreover, the copper ions modify the lining in the uterus, which considerably reduces the likelihood of implantation. Finally, abstinence--avoiding any intimate behaviors that could result in conception--is the only real form of contraceptive which has a 100% valid fee.

There are lots of factors that figure out the best contraception choices for any person. Some elements are usually related to individuality and habits. For instance, if a person is a forgetful man or woman, "the capsule" may not be her most suitable choice since it needs being taken each. Other variables that influence contraceptive choices include expense, age, education, spiritual beliefs, lifestyle, and sexual health and fitness

THE IMPORTANCE TO BE ABLE TO SHOW YOURSELF SEXUALLY

It seems quite evident that nowadays, as part of your before, the elderly seem scared of expressing themselves sexually. Females give the impact they are worried about revealing that facet to men. In exchange, men are concerned that when they disclose their intimate inner needs, they'll be viewed as anti-feminist. World and societal constructs happen to be emasculating men by blurring the outlines between your sexes. Media will be brainwashing individuals regularly, and for that reason, women appear wholly fed up of having to stay control of these relationships on each day to a day time frame in addition to not getting fulfilled in the bedroom.

I believe, when it comes to sexual behavior between two consenting men and women, nothing you need to taboo. I am aware that what of one partner are not actually what another few would favour but no person should experience inhibited in expressing their needs. I advocate making love ought to be liberating, intensive and caring but not all at precisely the same time. Plenty of unhappiness is due to inadequate, incompatible erotic partnerships. It had taken me quite a while to meet an individual I possibly could fulfil my carnal wishes with. I expended a long time, like others, sense guilty in what I came across arousing. I tried out to cover up it when several partner advised me that we were initially sordid or degenerate which indeed manufactured me feel unclean. But I continued to be unfulfilled sexually and in lots of the areas of my entire life when i lacked a channel in which expressing those desires. Given that I have a guy who is completely accepting and stimulating in every region of my life, i think a darkish cloud is raised, and my possible in the areas could be realised. I'm no more stifled.

Nobody gets the to disapprove of any intimate activities that are not harming other people, and indeed probably actually will assist in a persons wellbeing, health and basic positive lifestyle. By sharing exciting times, as well as your innermost sensation about your wishes, with your spouse, other areas of a relationship possess the opportunity to become healthy and rewarding. I'm not recommending that everyone should entail themselves in deviant making love, it wouldn't go well with all couples. Nevertheless, I do believe that people should □uery their lives should they feel they're unable to engage in out their wishes honestly with the individual they love.

Find out if the individual desires to have sex: This is the most vital part regarding an excellent sexual experience. If one of the partners is not 'in the mood' or does not desire to have sex it can lead to the entire process transforming sour. Here are sex placements Indian females like the most.

Kiss as well as caress: The very first step towards physical intimacy is kissing. The majority of females enjoy to kiss, and a passionate kiss can most definitely place her in the state of mind for some more. Also being close, kissing, touching and caressing your partner assists stimulate their erotic zones which will undoubtedly cause more pleasurable sex. It additionally results in a more robust sense of nearness as well as security-- 2 feelings that assist an individual to execute better in bed. So touch him/her, kiss and make your partner desired. This is additionally an additional way to help stop the individual's body picture concerns (if they have any), making them extra comfy in your existence.

A (8 actions to excellent foreplay).

Sexual activity. That little word in sex needs to be among the biggest misnomers. It recommends that what comes before penetrative intercourse is not the actual offer. For ladies, it's the main course.

WHY LADIES LOVE FOREPLAY.

Be ready: Sex is a beautiful thing. It's pleasant and also makes you feel happy. It likewise has a variety of various other health and wellness benefits like aiding you to burn calories and beating depression. It's no surprise that we are the only types that make love for satisfaction as well as not only procreation. Yet with all that enjoyable come troubles like unwanted pregnancies, STDs as well as emotional problems. So being prepared is your ideal option. Bring a prophylactic, have that birth control pill and keep in mind that you need to be emotionally all set for the act. Sex brings people more detailed. That's simply the means people are naturally made. So if you are preparing to have a one-night stand or are taking the initial step towards a fully committed partnership, to remember that you need to have your mind in sync with what your body desires. One excellent way to do this is to discuss it. Ask your companion if they have protection (if you don't, go out and buy some, there are a lot of alternatives to pick from), talk to him/her regarding what you believe this can cause and most significantly be honest concerning just how you regard the act (whether it is something you just wish to do for enjoyment with no strings attached or something a lot more severe.). Bear in mind; condoms are created once use. You can not utilise one prophylactic repetitively so see to it you get enough, just in case you plan to go at it more than as soon as. Find out more about five factors to have sex today!

WHY LADIES NEED SEXUAL ACTIVITY.

 Approach the individual gently as well as do not also seem desperate: Coming on too strong or being aggressive about having sex is one of the biggest turn-offs. Don't appear hopeless (even if you are passing away to be with the individual), permit the various other people some room to express their feelings. Sex needs to be a selection so allow them to choose.

It feels beautiful and also it fulfils a primal urge. It's a techni□ue of nature that the clitoris, females' Ground Zero of the orgasmic task, has actually been positioned outside the vaginal area and also out of straight contact with many of the activity.

Sex for women corresponds with the excitement of the clitoris, whether by a tongue, finger, helpful things like vibes, or every one of these concurrently - or by her partner's pubic bone in clitoris-friendly sex settings like The Grind. Yet equally, as a car engine re□uires to be heated up ade□uately in cold weather, it's ideal not to head right for this little bud. The more caring attention she gets in other places, the much more responsive she will be when the emphasis lastly changes to her genitals.

Choose the area as well as established the state of mind: Sex is an intimate act, at least it should be. So choose a place where both of you will be uninhibited, especially if it's your very first time. Pick a location that is private and has a comfortable position to make love in. An excellent soft bed with mood lights always aids the reason (unless you prepare to walk on an experimental path). So spend lavishly a little. Bear in mind enjoyment does come with a price.

Having sex can be a great deal of fun as well as gratifying, yet that being stated if you will try it for the first time and don't know where to start. Right here's a guide to assist you to understand that sexual code-- a detailed overview on exactly how to have sex.

STAGES OF SEX

A Step-By-Step Guide On How To Have Sex

Preparation to make love? Here is a step-by-step overview of the entire act

Men need an erection to have intercourse, and similarly, ladies' bodies re□uire to plan for infiltration. Sufficient foreplay ensures a female is excited as well as prepared for sex - the vagina balloons upwards and also outwards, and it generates lubrication to minimise rubbing and guarantee that sex is pleasurable. If she's not all set, sex may harm - and even the rubbing might trigger little rips in thc walls of her vagina, causing bleeding and even leaving her vulnerable to infection.

Early, women tend to uncover that the even more sexual activity they engage in, the higher the accumulate of sexual stress, resulting in much more extreme orgasms. The same commonly applies to men - the much longer he postpones culminating after repeatedly nearing the point of no return, a lot more eruptive his launch when he lastly releases. The more extended sexual activity lasts, the more probable females are to delight in several orgasms - as can men, when making use of methods to climax without climaxing.

Here is a guide to awesome sexual activity:

1. Take your time.

On average, women require about 20 minutes of foreplay to go from excited to orgasmic, whereas the majority of people take around three mins. Yet this is no collection policy as females' stimulation levels differ on a day-to-day basis - she might take an hr to climax today after a frantic day at the workplace, as well as just one min tomorrow after supper and sensual flick - as well as just how pairs engage additionally varies substantially.

2. Start slowly.

The areas outermost away from her genitals need to be focused on initial. A variant in the types of stimulation maintains her rate of interest ignited - from kisses as well as hot breaths to light touching, rubbing and also licking.

Differ feelings like temperature level with ice on her skin or cosy tea in your mouth.

3. Touch her skin.

Ladies like higher than only hands for sexual touching, like body-to-body caresses, the mouth and tongue, or massaging and also brushing with the pointer of the penis. Just like any excitement, a necessary regulation is to do it symmetrically - what you do away ought to more or less likewise be done to the opposite to produce a balance in stimulation.

4. Concentrate on less evident spots

Focusing on other erotic areas like her neck, toes, inner thighs, buttocks and also spine while staying clear of the hot spots of busts and also genital areas will certainly have the preferred impact of enhancing sensitivity in and even blood flow to her genitals.

5. Beginning outwards as well as work inwards

Begin by stimulating the outer areas of her breasts - the underside of the busts or her collarbone - and also delicately ease your way in the direction of the top with licks and strokes. Method her genital areas from the outskirts, progressively working your plan in.

6. Differ the excitement

As the nerve endings come to be much less sensitive with constant touch, the variant from light to firm strokes and also moving from one place to an additional makes sure the stimulation remains arousing.

7. Re□uest for comments

Women often tend to know what they enjoy in sexual activity yet might be reluctant in re□uesting for what they desire. What they value is a lover that asks if they're taking pleasure in the action as it advances, with in□uiries like "How does it feel if I do this.?" or "Would you like me to do this a little tougher or softer?" Excellent interaction and a determination to please in bed ensures a satisfied lover and also eventually, fantastic sex.

8. Method makes orgasmic

Probably one of the most fail-safe methods to be familiar with a female sexually and also lead her to repeat orgasms is to enjoy sex play without any penetration. Consider eradicating intercourse for a week or two and involving purely in various other types of sex-related interaction (shared oral sex, for instance) for a mind-blowing experience guaranteed to widen both your sex-related horizons. And when you do resume sexual intercourse, you'll have a restored appreciation for the pleasures of the trip there.

Pick the best moment: The right minute to have penetrative sex is generally really felt as well as is fre☐uently common. When your partner desires to move on to the next action, choose the minute. In some cases asking if the various other individual is ready or if he/she wants more is an excellent way to know when it's time. Once you know that he/she prepares, take it to the next level. Find out more regarding What's the best time of the day to make love?

Have a lot of foreplay: This is where you can either select to eliminate your clothing or have your partner undress you. Another method to deal with it is to remove one item of clothes at once, making the entire procedure an enigma. When it pertains to foreplay, most individuals think that sex is just penetrative. Yet the act does consist of sexual activity. Sexual activity, as the name recommends, is what you do before you make love. It includes caressing, kissing, stimulating your partner's erotic zones and foreplay too. Make sure you get sufficient of this in. Because the two of you can experiment with several techniques, it is fre□uently the most delightful part of the entire sexual experience. Pointer for males: Women can orgasm multiple times. So satisfaction your woman, she will undoubtedly be in the mood for some even more and thanks for it in more methods than one. The idea for women: Most guys love to be also touched, so make him feel great. Touch him, kiss him and feel his entire body. Do not keep back and also don't be the only one monopolising all the satisfaction.

Lovemaking: Once the first penetration is total, you can select to have sex; nevertheless, you both are comfy. Guy, make sure you drive (your penis into her vaginal area) in balanced motions as well as do it from the hip; this will guarantee your lady obtains the optimal pleasure. Allow yourself to really feel satisfaction and also make sure you take your partner's enjoyment right into consideration and also make her happy too.

Last couple of minutes: Once you both have culminated or the sex is regarding obtain over, you both will most possibly be in a state of happiness. Rushed sex can be amazing occasionally yet if it is done on a routine basis, it can leave you feeling a bit incomplete. Pointer for females: If you liked the experience, tell your companion that.

 Insertion: This is the most excited part regarding sex and is fre uently thought to be the only point that happens throughout it. If you are having safe sex, make sure you use a prophylactic before you put your penis right into her vaginal area. Several men get the placement wrong and often tend to 'look around' with their penis (attempt to pass through without understanding where the vaginal canal is) this can be excruciating for the lady.

Winding up: The coital message component can be beautiful in some cases and also unpleasant in others. So try to make your partner comfy. Give him/her a tee shirt to wear, flirt a little and also tell him/her exactly how good the experience was. Smile as well as share a laugh together. This could be the very best time to make a good friend or a companion forever. So make use of the possibility. After you'll are done, make sure you'll wash up. Ladies, wash your genital opening, as well as vulva and guys, must clean their penis once they get rid of the condom. Lastly, make sure you take care of the prophylactic properly. Do not flush it down the commode. Throw it in a dustbin wrapped in paper or tissue instead.

WHEN YOU HAVE YOUR PERIOD, BELOW ARE SEVEN REASONS TO GET IT ON.

1. It Helps Alleviate Cramps

This one likewise chooses when you're PMS-ing. A climax can aid nip those in the bud if you experience significant aches throughout your duration. When we orgasm, the body releases oxytocin and also dopamine, along with various other endorphins that can ease any period-related pains.

" While taking medication can assist minimise menstrual cramps, having an orgasm is an extra all-natural way to ease pain from the menstrual cycle," Dr Anna Klepchukova, MD, primary scientific research officer at Flo Health, tells Bustle. "This occurs because of endorphins. Dopamine, as well as serotonin, are launched during sex as well as can alter discomfort sensitivity, giving some remedy for cramping."

You may assume popping ibuprofen, or your preferred over-the-counter pain reliever will do the trick, as well as it can to a degree, but absolutely nothing is quite as powerful as a climax when it pertains to reducing pain.

Whether it's sex with a partner or sex with yourself, that climax is mosting likely to supply.

" Period sex can be untidy but, there are substantial benefits to making love while on your duration," reproductive endocrinologist and owner of Generation Next Fertility Dr Janelle Luk informs Bustle. "Sex can substantially reduce menstrual aches and pelvic pain by releasing endorphins that work as pain as well as stress and anxiety relief."

2. There's Less Need For Lube

If your vaginal area is on the dry side, or have a hard time producing enough lubrication naturally, then duration sex will likely be a welcome break from requiring lube. But before you start assuming the entire "ew, blood" point again, think of this: Yes, you're bleeding when you menstruate. However the majority of what you're seeing is the loss of your uterine lining.

" The hormone variations that happen during the duration cycle can cause women to have a higher libido, as well as numerous women, locate period sex more satisfying since there is no need for extra lubricating substance," Dr Luk states. "Even though lubrication might not be needed throughout period sex, females should still use defence because there is still a possibility that you could become pregnant or contract a sexually transmitted disease while on your duration."

On standard, females shed between 2 to 3 tbsps of blood each month. If you can justify just how very little the blood is and also focus on the positive-- the extra lube-- you may discover it more pleasurable.

3. You Probably Won't Find It, Gross

A 2012 research confirmed what anybody that's remained in the heat of the minute during their duration already recognises: Everything besides making love comes to be second. Researchers in the Netherlands located that sex-related arousal bypasses the natural disgust feedback, which suggests that when you begin, the truth that you're on your period may not also enter your mind.

In between an enhanced feeling of resistance for points that you 'd generally discover quite gross and an increased libido, it's safe to claim that the whole blood aspect may be very much from your mind. Specially when you add in the truth that sexes during your duration is incredible for cramps-- much better than any pill-- and also the lubrication factor. For women who experience painful sex, either as a result of friction or not being excited, the added slickness that comes with making love while menstruating can make sexual intercourse more pleasurable than it would certainly be otherwise.

" Your hormonal agent degrees are perfectly fit for a high libido during your duration," Schulte Wang says. "Progesterone is known to lower libido, and since that hormonal agent is the lowest at the beginning of your cycle, you may feel much more in the mood contrasted to other times of the month."

And after a few minutes, you'll also be active enjoying yourself and also as well excited to even care that blood becomes part of the e□uation.

4. It Can Shorten The Length Of Your Period

" During the climax, the uterus agreements, and also conse□uently blood may simply obtain pushed out much faster, and the circulation may seem a bit various," Dr Alyssa Dweck, OB/GYN, Assistant Clinical Professor at Mount Sinai School of Medicine, and writer of V is for Vagina, tells Bustle. "And [orgasm contractions pushing out] prostaglandins might have a function; they are secreted chemical substances responsible for menstruation cramps."

What this also means is that you don't have to make love with an additional person to reduce the size of your period. Self-pleasure, one of the very best means to pass the time as well as appreciate on your own, can also add to reduce your period-- as long as you orgasm, of course.

Yet not just will sex and also self-pleasure, thanks to climaxes, shorten the length of your period, yet it will also clear out the substances within the womb that are causing all that cramping as well as pressure, to begin with. Given, it's not an ensured method to reduce your duration, much like there's no guaranteed way to make your period come much faster. However it without a doubt does not hurt, and there are those powerful all-natural pain relievers that feature it, no matter what, to ensure that's something worth thinking about.

5. It Can Create Greater Intimacy

Although a January 2019 consumer research by The Flex Company discovered that 85% of ladies are much less likely to be intimate during their period, it doesn't need to be by doing this. You're permitting yourself to be vulnerable when you're ready to open up the floodgates and also have sex on your period. Vulnerability, even if it's something you're not 100% comfortable with, can make relationships more powerful.

" It can raise a lot of worry and anxiety to be prone and also open with your companion ...," certified psychologist, Jaclyn Witmer Lopez, informs Bustle. "Vulnerability is a massive factor to affection and link, so one has to combat need to shut it down."

To put it, making love on your duration is likewise opening the doors to much more profound affection in between you and also your partner. The more intimacy in a relationship, the better the link and even interaction. Having duration sex is primarily stating, "I would not allow simply any individual be this wrapped up in my blood, and also I can't picture you would certainly do this with simply anyone either."

6. It Will Break You Out Of Your Comfort Zone-.

If you're a missionary-in-bed-only sort of sex-haver, period sex may transform that. You might decide to attempt brand-new placements, or decide versus intercourse for other sex-related activities. According to Dr Dweck, sex in the shower is an alternative that some of her clients select when a companion is menstruating. Not even if it can conserve a precious collection of 1000-count Egyptian sheets, yet save a possible mess, although most likely minimal, too.

Yet, it must be noted that shower sex works much better in theory than in practice. Without the right ground, sex in the shower can be downright dangerous. For those that don't intend to risk shower sex, The Flex Company makes a non-reusable menstrual disc that works similar to a period mug in that it accumulates menstruation liquid, but it's put on at the base of the cervix, leaving your vagina open for organisation.

7. Because You Know You Want To.

But not just is there the need, yet with it comes enjoyment. Great deals of it. For some individuals, there's a deep desire to make love while they're menstruating and to indulge in that deep impulse makes sex even much better. It's like lastly giving in as well as scraping that irritating mosquito bite: it seems like absolute paradise.

" Many females experience more satisfying sex throughout their duration due to modifications in sex drive that occur naturally throughout the menstrual cycle," Dr Klepchukova states.

So if you have the desire to make love, after that, why on earth let a little blood stand in your way? Nevertheless, it's not like you allow your period to stop you from doing anything else.

People with periods often tend to be rather damn horny both best before and during their duration. The reason for this is that the pelvic location and also genitals obtain puffy, constructing arousal.

" There are some ladies who like to have sex during their duration, and also no wonder, our estrogen is normally at its lowest at the start of our period," sex instructor and also affection trainer, Elle Chase, tells Bustle. An increased horniness and enjoyment can become associated with period sex, magnifying sexual need.".

Split Level:

When the man is on leading, and the female has her legs spread wide with her knees curled up towards the guy's head, this is.

Did you understand that many couples discover it exciting and also really interesting to have sex in the kitchen? A quickie will make both of you excited sufficient to obtain right into even more activity in bed.

Hot Easy Ways to great Orgasms!

The adhering to guide includes some hot sex settings that will offer to make your love life more exciting and also enjoyable.

The Lap Position:

This is when the female rests atop the partner's lap as well as the man inserts his penis into her vagina. It can be a hard sexual placement to master however, it is delightful if you exercise it well as well as obtain your toughness going.

Cowgirl Style

While pregnant, the timeless woman ahead position proves to be most comfortable. In this setting, your companion must lie down on the bed, as well as you straddle him. You can control the rate, depth as well as the angle of infiltration throughout sex.

The Counter Top Position:

This is ranked as one of the best amongst the very best sex setting guide as it happens at the spur of the moment. She sits on the countertop while he inserts his penis at countertop height right into her vaginal area. It's one you do in the warmth of the moment with your enthusiast.

Spooning

This is an extremely safe sex placement to appreciate throughout pregnancy without any fears. Let your companion crinkles up behind you, and also you can cover your legs around the exterior of his legs.

THE SEX POSITIONS

BEST AND SAFE SEX POSITION DURING PREGNANCY

After that, there is no danger for the infant if the sex is regular. You might experience some mild contractions throughout orgasms however they are usually harmless

When it comes to sex throughout maternity, females are very nervous and have several concerns. While having sex, the couples become worried about the safety and security of the little one present in the womb that they stay clear of having sex.

Fireplace:

This is when a female is seated on an armchair, covering her legs and also arms around the man, that is stooping on the flooring in front of her. This is among the most effective sex placement overview for pair who are seeking a new revitalising climax.

Futon:

The female lies on her back at the edge of a table or futon or bed, covered by quilts as well as cushions. She spreads her legs wide open as well as the man kneels before her as well as enters her, standing up her legs with his shoulders. This raises the angle of penetration, however can be extremely pleasing for both.

The Wrap Around:

This is a genuinely passionate present according to the very best sex placement guide. The lady lies on her back and also the man rests on top of her. The woman wraps her legs around the man to feel more intensely the infiltration.

We understand that sex at the end of the day in the room comes to be uninteresting. As you whole, the hall after supper the bed looks so inviting to your tired eyes as well as a body that sleep is the only point you can think off. So, wait, do not intend to make love in the room if you are drop-dead weary. Break the monotony and get out of the bed. If you can have a quickie in the kitchen area, the best is. If you know, she is in the state of mind, just after you are done with your dinner, get into the cooking area. If your state, "Waiting for you in the bed, honey," you could sleep till she enters the room. Instead, like a devoted companion aid her in the cooking area and also obtain rowdy, talk dirty to her. Well, this techni□ue works even if you are in the state of mind as well as your lady is drop dead worn out from stabilising work and also house. Gently press her waist and get closer, whisper in her ears, attack them. Next off, enter the activity at the cooking area counter.

The Crawl or Doggy Style:

This popular sex setting places you both on your knees. The man inserts his penis right into her vaginal canal from behind and also makes love this way. It supplies excellent satisfaction and too intense sensations for both partners.

The baby in the womb continues to be bordered by amniotic fluid which safeguards it from any shock results. Nonetheless, the organ is above the vagina; hence infiltration doesn't get to there. If the sex is typical after that, there is no danger for the baby, you might experience some light contractions throughout climaxes; however they are generally harmless as well as there are a couple of good sex positions which can be enjoyed by the couple without the worry of any medical problems.

Side-by-side missionary position

In this position, both the partners face each other. The man can slip his legs over the woman as well as permeate from an angle. However, the person should be a bit less than the woman to help with infiltration. The woman can position her leading leg over his hip and the bottom one against his leg as a variant to this setting.

If you had a long tedious day at work opportunities are you don't want to obtain into activity in bed tonight. Sure she knows how to get you in the state of mind, so do not quit her as well as indeed a session of hot balmy sex will melt your stressors.

Head to Toe:

This is when the man lies on his back with his legs spread wide when he enters the woman. The woman lies down on her back with her legs spread across his, with her toes pointing toward his head and his head pointing away from hers.

Urgent:

This is for hot couples searching for top sex placements because the woman needs to stand with her legs wide open as well as supports herself with a chair or various other pieces of furniture. The man enters her from behind.

SHOWER SEX TIPS

Hit the showers with these tips to master shower sex like a boss and come out on the other side with no broken bones or bruised egos.

That said, shower sex has the potential to be the stuff of flicks with the best moves. It's a fun method to vapour points up-- literally-- as well as it can be a good break from the bedroom.

Swimming:

This is when the man pushes his back and also spreads his legs. The female then lies on top of him, consisting of putting her legs on his. The female regulates the drives by dragging her body backwards and forwards. This sex-related setting benefits great women orgasms.

Advantages And Precautions Of Spicing It Up With Shower Sex

When it pertains to bath sex, the only thing that's unsafe when damp is the shower flooring. This produces a potentially neck-breaking intermediary that isn't nearly as attractive as it is in the flicks. Anyone that's had shower sex, in reality, will most likely tell you it's, in fact, the most awful.

We've obtained settings, products, and also various other bits to assist you get your rub-a-dub on securely and also sexily.

1. Turn up the heat

Seriously. When you're cold, and you can bet your soggy bottom that at least one of you will be, it's hard to be hot. A showerhead can only cover so much ground, so turning up the heat beforehand will help.

2. Buy shower-friendly lube

Yes, water is wet, but it's not slippery lube wet. Reduce the friction and make vaginal or anal penetration easier with a silicone waterproof lube.

3. Invest in a non-slip shower mat

A non-slip bath mat is a must if you're planning to get sexy and sudsy at the same time. These grippy mats adhere to the bottom of your tub or shower and can be pulled up for cleaning when you're done getting dirty.

4. Rinse, then rinse some more

Lathering up your lover may be the epitome of romance in the movies, but soap, shampoo, and especially conditioner can make the shower floor extra slick. If you're going to lather up together, rinse well to get rid of any slimy residue. Also, soap is slippery, but it's not lube, so don't go there.

5. Bath toys

Bath toys aren't just for kids-- at least not the kind we're talking about. When it comes to waterproof sex toys like vibrating loofahs, waterproof vibrators, and butt plugs, you have some pretty impressive options.

6. Don't get stuck on penetration

Penetration isn't the holy grail of shower sex and doesn't need to be your focus or end game. The shower lends itself well to other kinds of play, including oral sex and exploring each other's erogenous zones.

SHOWER SEX POSITIONS

Virtually any sex position can be performed in the shower if you're determined enough, but that doesn't mean they're all a good idea. To keep from slip-sliding your way to the emergency room, give the following positions a try.

Pro tip: Get a suction shower handle or footrest for extra support during shower sex. They're affordable, reusable, and a lot sturdier and safer than the shower curtain or soap holder.

1. Standing doggy-style

This take on doggy lets you keep both feet firmly planted on the shower floor while you use your hands for extra support.

To do it:

Place your palms flat against the shower wall, leaning toward it with your knees slightly bent. This allows the other person to penetrate you from behind using a penis, sex toy, or fingers. They can also show your clitoris, perineum, or other bits some love.

2. Sit and ride

This works well for P in V sex, but can also work for anal penetration if you angle yourself just right.

To do it:

Have your partner sit on the floor of the shower, on the shower bench if you have one, or the side of the tub. Straddle them in any position that allows for penetration comfortably and hold on to them tight while you take a ride.

3. Get a leg up

Though not necessary, this is one position that would benefit from the footrest and handle we mentioned, but the side of a shower or the tub seat will do, too.

To do it:

Stand facing your partner and bring one leg up to the tub, bench, or footrest's edge. If you don't have any of those things, have your partner use one hand to hold your leg up while they thrust.

4. Got my back

This is similar to the leg up position, except with your back to your partner. It works for vaginal penetration from behind and anal penetration, too.

To do this:

Stand facing the shower wall and rest your foot on the tub, footrest, or bench's edge for support. Have your partner stand directly behind you and hold your leg up for extra comfort while they penetrate you.

5. The chairperson

This is like reverse cowgirl; only it can be used even with no cow or girl insight.

To do this:

What to consider and precautions

Shower sex can be precarious-- and we're not just talking about falls. Along with a non-slip mat and making sure you hold the wall, handle, or another sturdy surface for support, there are a few other things you should keep in mind.

Have your partner take a seat on the shower bench, the edge of the tub, or floor. Straddle their lap, facing away from them, positioning yourself for anal or vaginal penetration. Place your hands on their knees or against the shower wall for balance.

Takeaway

Fantastic shower sex is possible with some communication, care, and a little know-how.

Use condoms. Shower sex may be clean, but it won't protect you from STIs. Use condoms for penetrative sex and oral sex. A condom can also be cut to use as a dental dam for going down or rimming.

Shower sex isn't everyone's bag. Unless both parties consent and are totally into it, then you'll need to find another way to spice things up that you're both comfortable with.

Things get slippery outside the shower, too. Be careful when getting out of the shower or tub. Wet floors, floor mats, and bodies tangled in the throes of passion, making their way to the bedroom make tripping a severe possibility. Walk, don't run.

Staying wet too long can breed bacteria. Sorry to put a damper on your fun, but damp nether regions are a breeding ground for bacteria and fungi. Be sure to dry off thoroughly after shower sex to avoid a yeast infection.

Remember: Sex doesn't look the same for everyone, and intercourse in a shower is hard-- no pun intended. There are plenty of other things that can make for a pleasurable shower session.

Location a pillow under the hips if re□uired to aid bring the vaginal area up for more comfortable entry.

Dimension has nothing to do with skill when it involves sex BTW, that says sex is all about infiltration anyhow? Anyone with a penis-- real or of the store-bought variety-- can stick it in and out of an opening. Big whoop.

, if you're having penis-in-vagina sex.

If deeper infiltration is what you're after, the position makes all the distinction. It's worth keeping in mind that the vagina itself includes a restricted variety of nerve endings, particularly contrasted to the clitoris. So going deep shouldn't be your only focus.

To do it, the companion with the vagina pushes their back
and also drapes one leg over their companion's shoulder.
The permeating companion straddles the other leg and
enters them.

Doggy style

Since it uses up much deeper infiltration with a sexy view,
the Doggy design has stood the examination of time.

WHAT DO YOU MEAN BY "SMALL"?

Based upon the results of the most current research study of
over 15,000 individuals, the typical penis length is 3.6 in
(9.1 cm) while flaccid and 5.2 in (13.1 centimeters) while
putting up.

Below are some settings to attempt that will take P-in-V
sex to, cough, a much deeper level of pleasure. So every
person obtains a little somethin', we include placements for
all skill and convenience degrees.

Vaginal canal on top

Much better referred to as "cowgirl," this begins with the partner with the penis lying on their back while the various other partner climbs on encountering them.

A boost

This position gets legs out of the way for full get in touch with penetration while offering both parties simple accessibility to the clit for optimal enjoyment.

Anxious regarding just how you measure up? Do not be. While 15,000 may feel like a lot, it's just a spit in the sea when you consider that the existing worldwide male populace is close to 3.9 billion.

This enables the deep infiltration, as well as the companion on the top, can ensure the penis stays in for the entire trip by utilizing a grinding or side-to-side movement as opposed to only going up and down.

Reward: Grinding as close as you can obtain additionally reveals the clitoris some simultaneous love.

The partner with the vagina jumps on all fours while their partner kneels as well as enters them from behind. For an even deeper dive, the person being passed through should lower their head and also upper body down onto the bed while arching their back.

HOW TO HAVE TERRIFIC SEX WITH A SMALLER-THAN-AVERAGE PENIS

Points to consider

Is bigger far better? If you're speaking about a tub of ice lotion, specific--. In connection with the penis dimension, not a lot.

All that said, if you intend to make more of what you've obtained-- whatever that might be-- some placements enable much deeper infiltration than others. We'll cover those, plus various other pointers to assist you up to your sex video game overall.

In-person

A setting that gets all your most popular components touching, enables some seriously attractive eye call, and constructing out? Yes, please!

When attempting these moves, be sure to use a whole lot of lube as well as go super slow.

Missionary anal

This timeless P-in-V position is additionally extremely butt-friendly.

To begin, the recipient lies on their back with their knees pulled right into their breast. Making use of a pillow underneath can help elevate all-time low even higher.

Pile vehicle driver

Some severe adaptability and a rug or covering on the flooring are needed for this innovative step.

A smaller sized appendage and rectal sex is a match made in paradise.

If you get the angle just right, promoting the A-spot is a sporting chance. And also, the getting companion can get to down and play with their clitoris at the same time.

Rectal heap driver

This is similar to the P-in-V stack vehicle driver discussed above; just it's the anus being permeated.

This delicate location teems with very sensitive nerve endings and also some fragile skin. If you're not stretched or sufficiently prepped for rectal, also a smaller-than-average penis can tear you a new one.

With the getting partner on all fours, the giver can conveniently boost their companion's anus using a well-lubed finger before stooping behind and putting their penis.

Plank

This is a whole lot like missionary, except the companion being passed through gets on their belly. The penetrating partner gets into a plank placement over leading and also enters them from behind.

To start, the partner with the vaginal area rests on their back as well as swings their boosts and back over their head, so their feet areas near the flooring as possible. Next, the companion with the P squats over the top as well as enters them, crouching to embed and also out.

The angle created by this setting shows the front wall of the vaginal canal some significant lovin', which happens to be where the G-spot is located.

, if you're having penis-in-anus sex

Doggy style

This is by far (ha!) the most comfortable position for anal infiltration as well as suitable for newbies.

Seesaw

For the sophisticated backdoor gamer, the seesaw position lets the receiver take the lead in propelling, so they can make it as deep as they want.

The companion doing the passing through rests on the bed with legs expanded as well as hands behind them for support. Next, the obtaining companion sits on their lap facing them and also puts their hands behind them, so their hands are hing on their partner's legs.

To evaluate: The getting companion lies on the floor and also brings their upper hands and even over, next to their head. The penetrating partner crouches over leading as well as get in, using a squatting movement to thrust in and out.

Next off, the partner with the penis settings themselves over their companion, and also they both relocate together to find the very best angle for penetration.

For this, the companion with the penis sits on the end of the bed or a chair. The partner with the vaginal canal straddles their lap for access. Wrap your arms around each other as well as bone up.

The elegance of this position is that the recipient's legs are flat on the bed and also extended, producing a tight space for the penis to press right into. The tightness of the area feels great for the provider, while the recipient's sure to love that complete sensation.

The giver rests on their back, and the receiver straddles their faces. The receiver can deal with ahead for P or V dental, or turn a cheek to the provider for a rectal tongue lashing.

This position works for sex toy play and also handbook excitement like handjobs and fingering, as well as cunnilingus, strike work, and rimming.

Why restrict oral sex as well as erotic fun to foreplay? With its orgasmic possibility and also versatility, both deserve primary event condition. Tickles, tongues, and even toys, oh my!

Open wide

This setting is best suited to giving dental to a person with a penis, yet with a little tweaking-- instead, crouching-- you could make it benefit a vaginal area or anus, also

You can provide someone a BJ in this setting, as well. Just put a pillow in between their legs to prop up your head to obtain you closer.

Below are some moves for all ability levels that are worth a try, despite the penis dimension.

Butterball

The fortunate recipient lies on their back with their knees pulled right into their upper body, fittingly appearing like a turkey ready for great basting. Their partner, after that, lays belly-down ahead of the spread so they can tongue the clit, penis, and also spheres, or anus easily.

Lie back as well as take pleasure in

The getting companion lies back with a cushion under their butt as well as legs apart and appreciates the feel as well as the sight.

Doggy

Great ol' doggy style does it once again.

The giver rests on their bed with their neck at the edge as well as head hanging back. Their companion towers above them, placing their scrap over their partner's open mouth. Teabag, anybody?

In your face

We're entering into facesitting region currently. Some people find it a little claustrophobic, while others like the kinky element.

The receiver hops on all fours, and the giver behind has all of it right in their face and all set for cunnilingus or rimming.

69

You either love it or despise it, however the 69 shares the pleasure similarly between partners.

A single person lies on their back and the various other climbs on, facing their partner's feet so you're both up close and individual with the other's genitals.

Got mad oral abilities and also muscle strength? Attempt a standing 69.

If you're much less endowed, things to keep in mind

Certain, the globe's got its share of size queens, but ask most individuals concerning their finest sex ever before as well as dimension hardly ever obtains a mention. Chemistry, excitement, as well as steps are what make an experience remarkable.

You'll desire to be on top to obtain the angle right for your companion if rectal play is your enjoyment.

Below are some do's and also do n'ts to remember for you following sack sesh if you're bothered with your penis size:

Don't contrast yourself to others. Based upon study, 85 percent of individuals who have a penis overestimate the ordinary dimension, thinking that everybody else is packing a much larger piece.

Do be confident, even if you have to fake it till you make it. Confidence truly is attractive, as well as emphasizing regarding your penis dimension will ruin sex faster than a smaller-than-average penis. Exercise confidence-building strategies like positive self-talk to obtain you there.

Do not be afraid to use props and also toys. And also, adding toys makes you look like a proficient as well as certain badass in the bed room.

Do boost your hip flexibility. This will certainly allow for much deeper infiltration and make you a master thruster. Usage basic hip stretches to limber you up.

If your partner is much less gifted, things to maintain in mind

Penises can be found in all shapes and sizes, some smaller sized than others. Right here are some do's and do n'ts to bear in mind if your companion is much less gifted:

Do not exist. Unless you're engaging in roleplay they have actually consented to, acting as well as lying like they have a huge penis can do more injury than excellent to your connection and their confidence.

Do hold your horses. Penis anxiousness is as real as other sorts of negative body image issues. It may take time for your companion to become comfy in their very own skin as well as with you.

Don't fake it. Fabricating an O isn't the solution if it's just not working for you. You both should have to have gratifying sex. Experiment with various other methods and also interact honestly about what help you and what doesn't.

Don't ask if it's in. For noticeable factors, asking if it's in is a no-no. Get to down for a feeling to be certain if you're really not sure.

The bottom line

A huge penis isn't required for earth-shattering sex, yet self-confidence, interaction, as well as a readiness to attempt new things are.

The key to any excellent experience is maximizing what you have. Certain placements, concentrating on more than simply penetration, as well as using toys can make all the difference.

WHAT DO YOU MEAN BY "BIG"?

According to the most recent research on penis size, the average penis length is 3.6 in (9.16 centimeters) while drooping as well as 5.2 in (13.12 cm) while erect.

HOW TO HAVE GREAT SEX WITH BIGGER-THAN-AVERAGE PENIS

Things to think about

Even though penis size doesn't determine how good the sex is going to be, individuals still buy into the misconception that larger is far better when it comes to the D. That is till they've got one staring them down in the face.

Relying on just exactly how large we're chatting, making love with a bigger-than-average penis can have its challenges. Lucky for you, fantastic sex isn't just about penetration, and even if you do wan na ride the monster, there are means to make it easier.

As far as girth, the ordinary area is 3.7 in (9.31 centimeters) while flaccid and 4.6 in (11.66 cm) while erect. To be taken into consideration bigger than standard, you 'd re□uire to measure significantly bigger.

IF YOU'RE HAVING PENIS-IN-VAGINA SEX

If you or your partner is particularly well-endowed, give these a ride. To cover all the bases, we've consisted of settings for all skill degrees. You're welcome.

The possibility of sticking something actually big in the vaginal canal may be a little daunting, but it's not impossible. The trick is to find means to make it feel helpful for all entailed. That's where we come in.

Side-by-side

It's like spooning just you're facing each other. The setting itself restricts how deep the penis can go, and if that's not enough, the partner being passed through can maintain their legs directly for also shallower penetration.

To do it, both celebrations push their side facing the same direction with the well-endowed partner spooning from behind.

Limited missionary

When getting banged missionary-style, the partner with the V can regulate how much of the D they obtain by keeping their legs together.

To keep points unsafe as well as wet, simply get to down as well as play with your clit utilizing your hand or a small vibrator.

Spooning

It's intimate, enchanting, and most of all, it does not permit very deep infiltration. It's the ideal position for some attractive neck kissing as well as leaves hands complimentary to satisfaction various other spots.

To do it, assume the common penis-on-top position, just the partner being permeated maintains their legs within their companion's legs. This creates a tight squeeze that feels like being done in to the penetrator, while providing the receiver just enough.

The placement is high on intimacy as well as best for individuals that enjoy to kiss-- and that does not?

Standing doggy

Doggy style with a large member could be a harsh trip with an overzealous companion. Standing dog, on the other hand, makes deep infiltration a little, ahem, harder.

Vaginal area on the top

Yes, this set's usually recommended for sex with a smaller-than-average penis. The idea of riding a beast dick might seem nuts, however bear with me for a sec.

The reason this setting works is that it permits the companion with the vagina to regulate the depth-- with a little care, naturally.

Simply straddle your partner who needs to be level on their back and utilize your legs and also hands to manage your trip.

To do it, the companion with the V stands encountering a wall surface for assistance while their companion enters them from behind. It may take a little squatting or tippy-toe action to get the angle ideal, making this a little an advanced relocation.

IF YOU'RE HAVING PENIS-IN-ANUS SEX

The rectum is already rather tight quarters, yet toss a bigger penis into the mix and things can obtain truly unpleasant and also harmful.

Easy biker

This is basically the rectal sex variation of the vaginal area on the top setting. The celebration with the P pushes their back as well as the receiving partner gets on facing them.

Promoter

P-in-V missionary could enable deep infiltration, yet the D's obtained more exterior space to overcome to get to the rectum. This creates shallower penetration.

To do it, the obtaining companion lies facedown with their legs spread. The giver then pushes top additionally facedown but facing their partner's feet. This leaves you virtually butt-to-butt with the penis resting simply over for anal entrance.

Butt-to-butt

We're reaching pornography star ability level below, but still keeping the large D in mind. This setting puts the penis at a down angle that can be a little bit complicated, which is why it works for anal with a big one.

To drive, both companions press forwards and also backwards right into each other.

If you're not extra mindful, splits-- of the skin and also the crying-in-pain kind-- are feasible.

Because the recipient gets to control the depth using their hands and also knees for support, this placement functions.

Reverse easy motorcyclist

Yup, it's reverse cow for anal-loving peeps. Similar to the setting above, the permeating partner exists level on their back, just this time the recipient of the huge D climbs on facing the various other instructions.

So what's an anal-loving individual to do? Attempt a few of these big-D-friendly placements. Just bear in mind to go specifically sluggish as well as make use of massive ⬜uantities of lube. Training making use of playthings to stretch your anus first is a great concept if you're brand-new to rectal.

Resting canine

Ouch-free dog with a bigger dick is feasible with this adjustment. As opposed to getting on all fours for penetration, the receiver lies level on their stomach with their legs straight and also together.

The receiving companion rests on their back and also the passing through partner hovers above and enters in between their partner's a little parted legs. Don't neglect to get to down and reveal the genital areas some like to keep you aroused and your sphincter relaxed.

The permeating partner pushes top and also enters from behind. The shut legs as well as angle help limit exactly how deep they can go without eliminating from the pleasure.

Have the companion under bend their knees so the cyclist has something to keep to assist manage the deepness. As Well As Big D-- delight in the view!

If you're having erogenous or oral enjoyable

When really feeling charitable, the recipient can swap settings with their companion and return the support.

FYI: You can stay clear of the gag when offering a huge participant a beej by covering your hands around the base of their shaft as well as taking simply the suggestion right into your mouth.

The body's loaded with sensitive areas deserving of exploration, consisting of the rectal and also genital area, of course.

Have a seat

Similar to the name suggests, the lucky recipient takes a seat on the edge of the bed or a chair and also spreads their legs.

The partner on the receiving end of the stimulation exists back on the bed while their companion does all the job. By job, we mean kissing and caressing their erogenous areas, dental, rimming, or sex plaything play.

Mix it up with feeling play using your mouth, hands, props, and also playthings, and trying out various positions like these.

The well-endowed member gets on top of their companion who's lying face down as well as slides their lubed shaft backwards and forwards between their companion's ass cheeks.

Take it to one more level by having one or both events put on a butt plug during play. Placing a vibrator under their vulva offers them something hot to grind on if the partner on the bottom has a vagina.

Penetrative sex is NOT the holy grail of sex by any stretch. Foreplay and erogenous fun can up your chances of an orgasm as well as give those sore genital areas a much-needed as well as oh-so-pleasurable break.

Their partner kneels in between and also can use their mouth, hands, toys, or all of the above to function them into a frenzy. Make this setting butt play-friendly by having the recipient lean back while the provider puts their hands under their butt to bring it closer.

Lie back and take pleasure in

So basic, yet so flexible.

Slide 'n slide

This position gives all the feels of penetration without needing to get it in.

Dog

Is this placement ever flexible! Whoa!

Below are things to take into consideration that can assist save you from discomfort and also make the best of sex with your large good friend.

With one partner on all fours, the various other partner can kneel behind or even lay just below for access to every one of their partners most wonderful little bits.

You can master the beast with placements that feel impressive without going unfathomable and also by creating crazy non-penetrative sex skills. Include great deals of lube and also have a good time!

Here are some points to remember that can make sex with a bigger penis better for you and also your companion.

With their partner on all fours, the provider can delight in rimming, execute a strike task or vaginal dental, or use a vibe on any kind of part of their body. Anal or genital penetration with fingers as well as playthings is likewise on the menu right here-- as long as they consent, natch.

THINGS TO REMEMBER IF YOU'RE MORE GIFTED

When you're specifically well-endowed, you can not just go tossing that thing around all willy-nilly. A little prep work and finding out to collaborate with what you've got is vital.

In your face

Like some kink? This setting includes facesitting, which isn't for everyone.

Make certain you're using the ideal condom dimension. Pressing right into a prophylactic that's as well small resembles attempting to cram your dimension 32 bottom into dimension 28 skinny denims---- a mishap waiting to take place. Pick prophylactics made for larger sizes, like Trojan Magnum Bareskin Condoms, to avoid the dreadful damaged prophylactic dilemma.

Always have lube on hand. Lube is a large cock's-- and its partner's-- finest close friend.

Use penis rings. Penis rings can provide some great brand-new experiences for both while also protecting against the cock from going in right. Then there are rings like the Oh Nut and Come Close Pleasure Ring, which are particularly designed to stop deep thrusting as well as aid regulate depth.

Lube, lube, lube! Lube makes sex easier and also safer by decreasing rubbing, which can aid stop skin tears that enhance your threat of STIs.

Stay with positions that keep you in control-- at the very least at first. Up until you and also your partner find your rhythm and learn what jobs, select front/rear-entry placements that place you in control of the drive.

Work that pelvic flooring. If you have a vaginal canal, reinforcing your pelvic flooring may make it easier to fit their dimension. Pelvic floor exercises like Kegels are an excellent beginning.

The bottom line

A bigger-than-average penis can be a bit hard to take, literally.

This setting might be a little too deep throat-friendly as well as bit much for their partner's mouth if the huge D is on top.

IF YOUR COMPANION IS EXTRA ENDOWED, THINGS TO KEEP IN MIND

In the company of a big 'un? Some might high five you, but we feel your discomfort.

To do it, the partner being rested on lies on the bed with their directly a cushion as well as the various other individual straddles their face. The face-sitter can lean back or ahead to angle themselves for a blow task, genital oral, or rimming.

As opposed to a full-on BJ, gliding the penis backward and forward over their companion's damp lips and tongue can be equally as hot.

Pro-tip: if you cut a prophylactic up the side, you can open it out and put it over the vulva for more secure foreplay there. Prophylactics are handy for everybody!

Prophylactics are the only sort of birth control out there that likewise help protect versus STDs. So even if you're making use of another form of birth control (like the pill), it's an excellent idea to likewise utilize condoms to stop the spread of sexually transmitted infections.

Keep in mind that condoms made of lambskin or various other pet membranes DO NOT protect versus STDs-- they only avoid pregnancy. Only artificial condoms (latex or plastic) prevent the spread of STDs.

How does the dental implant work?

The birth control dental implant is a small, slim pole
regarding the size of a matchstick. It's also called
Nexplanon as well as there's a somewhat older variation
called Implanon. A physician inserts the implant under the
skin of your upper arm. It launches the hormonal agent
progestin to stop you from obtaining expecting.

EXCELLENT AND ALSO MUCH SAFER SEX

WHAT IS A CONDOM?

Prophylactics are slim, stretchy bags that you wear on your penis during sex. Condoms give wonderful protection from both maternity and also STDs. They're easy to use and also simple to get.

Lambskin prophylactics do not safeguard versus STDs. Only latex and plastic condoms do.

What's a prophylactic and exactly how does it function?

Prophylactics are small, thin bags made of latex (rubber), plastic (nitrile, polyurethane, or polyisoprene) or lambskin, that cover your penis during sex as well as collect semen (orgasm). Condoms stop sperm from getting into the vagina, so sperm can't meet an egg and also create maternity.

Condoms likewise protect against STDs by covering the penis, which stops contact with sperm as well as genital liquids, and also limits skin-to-skin get in touch with that can spread sexually transferred infections.

Do prophylactics assist protect versus STDs?

Yes! Using condoms whenever you have oral, anal, or genital sex is the very best means to reduce your possibilities of obtaining or spreading sexually transmitted infections. Condoms shield you as well as your companions from STDs by avoiding contact with physical fluids (like sperm and genital fluids) that can bring infections. And because prophylactics cover your penis, they help protect versus particular STDs like herpes and genital blemishes that are spread out via skin-to-skin get in touch with (but they're rather much less efficient with these since they do not cover all your skin).

The hormonal agents in the birth control dental implant avoid pregnancy in 2 means:

Does the implant prevent STDs?

Nope. Nexplanon does not protect versus STDs. Fortunately, utilizing prophylactics or internal condoms every time you have sex does reduce your opportunities of getting or spreading STDs. So making use of prophylactics with your dental implant is the best method to prevent infections

Progestin thickens the mucous on your cervix, which stops sperm from swimming through to your egg. When sperm can't meet up with an egg, maternity can't happen.

SAFER SEX

In the grand system of points, you might be stunned to hear, staying clear of sex is damaging to your mental and physical well-being-- whereas, having sex can be widely helpful (Charnetski & Brennan, 2004; Ditzen, Hoppmann & Klumb, 2008; Hall et al., 2010). Much safer sex involves reviewing as well as using obstacles-- male condoms, women prophylactics, or dental dams-- relative to your certain sex-related habits. Maintain in mind: Although safer sex may make use of some of the very same tools as birth control, much safer sex is not birth control.

If you choose you desire to get expecting or you just don't want to have your dental implant any longer, your medical professional can take it out. You can keep track of your insertion as well as elimination days utilizing our birth control app.

Progestin can additionally □uit eggs from leaving your ovaries (called ovulation), so there's no egg to feed. When eggs aren't released, you can't get pregnant.

Nevertheless, the most common root cause of dry penile skin is as simple as rubbing. This might be brought on by masturbating without a lube, apparel rubbing on the penis, or delicate penile skin being aggravated throughout sexual relations.

If you swim regularly in a chlorinated pool or at the coastline, then maybe you require to take into consideration shielding your penis skin with a water-repelling lotion or cream prior to swimming to stop the chemicals or salt hopping on your penis.

If you have a penis piercing, see as well as get rid of the ring if this makes a difference to the problem of your skin. You might find that you have an allergy to the steel located in the ring; and also.

SEXUAL DYSFUNCTION

DRY PENIS

Dry penis epidermis can be the effect of a number of causes according to medical professionals, such as for example sexual action, an allergic attack to latex, and perhaps sexually transmitted disorders, eczema, and psoriasis or skin area cancer.

However, the most frequent reason behind dry penile skin area is as easy as friction. This can be due to masturbating with out a lubricant, garments rubbing around the penis, or very sensitive penile skin staying annoyed during sexual intercourse.

Therefore before starting to be worried about the much more serious conditions, such as for example STD's or skin area cancer, that may be drying your skin layer consider using an activity of elimination, and perhaps using a exceptional penile epidermis moisturizer.

Below are a few basic dry penis pores and skin solutions for you yourself to try, before you decide to consult your medical professional:

Consider switching your soap to 1 that's for sensitive skin area;

Try using another brand of cleansing natural powder or detergent for the clothing;

Use a cloth softener if you're not currently making use of one, or adjust the brand you utilize to one that's for sensitive skin area;

Consider using underwear that's made from various material. For instance, if you use satin g-strings or boxers you'd like to try cotton types;

If you don no underwear next start using some;

Buy a exceptional penis moisturizing product or service that soothes and revitalizes penis epidermis, and is developed specifically for your penis. The product should contain vitamin products, mineral deposits, and antioxidants which are penis skin particular which means that your penis skin is definitely nourished and in a position to rejuvenate;

Change your make of condom, if you are using them during sexual intercourse;

Purchase a lubricant that you could apply just before, and during sex, to avoid penis skin discomfort;

Wash the hands before and after coming in contact with your penis;

If you are using a body-wash subsequently stop by using this;

Consider altering the make of your genital deodorant, or any health products that you utilize;

When you have a penis piercing, take away the ring and find out if this is important to the health of your skin. You might find to have an allergic attack to the metallic within the wedding ring; and

In the event that you swim regularly within a chlorinated pool area or at the beachfront, then perhaps you need to think of guarding your penis pores and skin using a water-repelling ointment or ointment before swimming to avoid the chemical substances or salt having on your own penis.

Work the right path through this record systematically, attempting one solution following the other, and soon you find the appropriate solution for you personally, or and soon you have tried all of them. Give each choice at the least 2-3 days or more to weekly to work prior to trying the next answer. And, if after hoping these simple alternatives you still discover that you may have dry penis pores and skin, then it really is highly recommended you consult your medical doctor.

WHAT'S TO LEARN ABOUT ERECTILE DYSFUNCTION?

A man is known as to possess erectile dysfunction if he on a regular basis finds it challenging getting or retaining a firm plenty erection in order to possess sex, or if it inhibits other sexual exercise.

Most men own occasionally seasoned some difficulty making use of their penis becoming difficult or staying company. Even so, erectile dysfunction (ED) is considered a problem if acceptable sexual performance has become impossible on several occasions for quite a while.

Since the finding that the medicine sildenafil, or Viagra, impacted penile erections, a lot of people have become conscious that ED is really a treatable condition.

Men who've a problem making use of their sexual performance could be reluctant to talk to their doctor, viewing it could be an embarrassing concern.

Fast information on erectile dysfunction:

Erectile dysfunction (ED) means persistent difficulty reaching and keeping an erection satisfactory to possess sex.

Causes are often medical but may also be psychological.

Organic causes are often the conse□uence of an underlying condition affecting the arteries or nerves offering the penis.

Numerous prescription medications, recreational drugs, li□uor, and using tobacco, can all produce ED.

CAUSES

Normal erectile work can be afflicted with problems with the following methods:

• blood flow

• nerve supply

• hormones

• Physical causes

It will always be worth consulting with a physician about continual erection problems, since it could be the effect of a serious condition.

Whether the result in is easy or serious, an authentic diagnosis can help address any actual medical problems and help fix sexual difficulties.

The list following summarizes some of the most frequent physical or organic and natural factors behind ED:

• Cardiovascular disease and narrowing of arteries

• diabetes

• raised blood pressure

• high cholesterol

• excess weight and metabolic syndrome

• Parkinson's disease

• multiple sclerosis

• hormonal disorders adding thyroid problems and testosterone deficiency

• structural or anatomical problem from the penis, such as for example Peyronie disease

• using tobacco, alcoholism, and drug abuse, consisting of cocaine use

• therapies for prostate disease

• surgical complications

• injuries within the pelvic spot or spinal-cord

• radiation therapy for the pelvic region

Atherosclerosis is really a common reason behind blood flow troubles. Atherosclerosis will cause a narrowing or clogging of arteries inside the penis, avoiding the necessary blood circulation for the penis to create an erection.

Numerous prescription drugs can also trigger ED, including those beneath. Anyone taking prescription drugs should seek advice from their medical professional before preventing or altering their medications

• drugs to regulate raised blood pressure

• heart medications such as for example digoxin

• some diuretics

• drugs that function on the fundamental nervous system, consisting of some sleeping capsules and amphetamines

• anxiety treatments

• antidepressants, adding monoamine oxidase inhibitors (MAOIs), selective serotonin reuptake inhibitors (SSRIs), and tricyclic antidepressants

• opioid painkillers

• some cancer tumor drugs, incorporating chemotherapeutic agents

• prostate remedy drugs

• anticholinergics

• hormone drugs

• the peptic ulcer treatment cimetidine

Physical causes take into account 90 percentage of ED circumstances, with psychological factors much less popular.

PSYCHOLOGICAL CAUSES

In rare circumstances, a guy may will have had ED and could never have realized an erection. That is called principal ED, and the reason is almost generally psychological when there is no noticeable anatomical deformity or physiological matter. Such psychological variables range from:

• guilt

• concern with intimacy

• depression

• severe anxiety

Most situations of ED are usually 'extra.' Which means that erectile function have been normal, but gets problematic. Factors behind a fresh and persistent trouble are usually actual.

Less commonly, emotional factors result in or donate to ED, with variables which range from treatable mental well being illnesses to each day emotional states that a lot of people experience sometime.

You will need to note that there may be overlap between medical related and psychosocial factors. For instance, in case a man is fat, blood flow alterations make a difference his capability to manage an erection, which really is a physical cause. Nevertheless, he may likewise have low self-esteem, that may impact erectile work and is really a psychosocial cause.

DOES OPERATING A BICYCLE PRODUCE ED?

Questions remain concerning the outcomes on men's health and fitness of driving a bicycle.

Some research possesses raised considerations that men who on a regular basis cycle for extended hours could have an increased threat of ED, along with other men's medical issues such as for example infertility and prostate cancer tumor.

The newest study to research this discovered that there is no hyperlink between buttoning a shirt and ED, nonetheless it did find a link between longer time of bicycling and the chance of prostate tumor.

Prostate sickness and ED

Prostate cancer will not cause ED.

Even so, prostate surgery to eliminate the tumors and radiation remedy to take care of prostate cancer could cause ED.

Therapy of non-cancerous, benign prostate condition can also result in the condition.

TREATMENT

Fortunately that we now have many solutions for ED, & most men will see a remedy that works for these people. Treatments contain:

Drug treatments

Men may take several drugs referred to as PDE-5 (phosphodiesterase-5) inhibitors.

Many of these pills are used 30 to 60 mins before sex - the very best known staying the blue-colored supplement sildenafil (Viagra). Additional options are:

• vardenafil (Levitra)

• tadalafil (obtained as a once-daily supplement called Cialis)

• avanafil (Stendra)

PDE-5 inhibitors are just available on doctor prescribed. A health care provider will look for heart conditions and have about other prescription drugs being considered before prescribing.

Side-effects connected with PDE-5 inhibitors consist of:

• flushing

• visual abnormalities

• hearing loss

• indigestion

• headache

Less popular drug options contain prostaglandin E1, that is utilized locally by either injecting it in to the penis or placing it down the starting of this urethra.

Most men like a pill, nevertheless, so these locally operating drugs are usually reserved for men who cannot consider oral treatment.

Online pharmacies

You'll be able to buy treatment online for ED. On the other hand, caution is preferred.

AMERICA (U.S.) Meals and Drug Supervision (FDA) includes a consumer safety guidebook about this, like a recommendation to check on that the web pharmacy:

• is situated in the U.S. and licensed

• has a accredited pharmacist to take questions.

• requires a doctor prescribed.

• offers direct connection with someone who can go over any problems.

• You can examine if the pharmacy is accredited using this set of Verified Web Pharmacy Practice Web sites (VIPPS).

The FDA offers strategies for spotting the hazards of an unsafe webpage, including observing out for the next clues:

• There is absolutely no way to make contact with the web site by phone.

• Prices are greatly less than those provided by legitimate online pharmacies.

• Prescription drugs can be found without demanding a doctor prescribed - that is illegal.

• Personal information isn't protected.

• The FDA brings that these outlawed sites may give drugs of undiscovered □uality and source, even sending the incorrect drug or perhaps a dangerous product.

Vacuum devices

Vacuum erection gadgets are a mechanised way of delivering an erection for men who usually do not desire or cannot work with prescription drugs, or find they're not working.

The penis is manufactured rigid through a vacuum pump motor closed around it that attracts up blood. That is prevented from after that allowing the penis through an accompanying strap.

Having less spontaneity by using vacuum devices implies that many men get other solutions for ED more suitable.

Surgical treatments

There are many surgical treatment choices:

Penile implants: They are a final alternative reserved for men who've not experienced any results with prescription drugs along with other non-invasive options.

Vascular surgery: Another medical option for a few men is definitely vascular surgery, which makes an attempt to improve some bloodstream vessel factors behind ED.

Surgery is really a last resort and can only be utilized in probably the most acute cases. Recovery period varies, but accomplishment rates are large.

Do health supplements and alternative solutions work?

The short response is certainly "no."

No guidelines accompanied by medical doctors, nor any set up sources of facts, support the usage of dietary supplements, such as for example herbal pills.

Along with there staying no evidence and only non-prescription options for ED, the FDA possesses warned of invisible dangers of "treatments" offered online.

Symptoms

Men might not always successfully gain an erection, and when this rarely takes place, it isn't considered a skilled problem.

However, ED will not only make reference to a complete lack of ability to attain an erect penis. Signs can also involve struggling to keep up an erection for extended enough to perform intercourse or an incapability to ejaculate.

There are normally also emotional signs, such as shame, shame, stress and anxiety, and a lower life expectancy fascination with sexual intercourse.

A man is known as to possess ED when these signs occur regularly.

Exercises

There are workouts a guy can perform to reduce the conse uences of ED.

The ultimate way to handle erectile dysfunction without treatment is by conditioning the pelvic ground muscle groups with Kegel workout routines. These are typically connected with women seeking to fortify their pelvic location during pregnancy, however they can be powerful for men seeking to regain full purpose from the penis.

Firstly, discover the pelvic floor muscle tissue. You can accomplish that by ending mid-stream several times next time you urinate. The muscle mass you can sense working in this process will be the pelvic floor muscle tissue, and they'll be the concentrate of Kegel workouts.

One Kegel workout consists of tightening up and positioning these muscle tissues for 5 mere seconds and then launching them. Make an effort to carry out between 10 and 20 repetitions every day. It isn't really possible when you initially start performing the exercises. However, they ought to become easier as time passes.

You ought to be able to recognize a noticable difference after 6 days.

Be sure you are breathing in a natural way throughout this technique and avoid forcing down just like you are usually forcing urination. Rather, bring the muscle tissues together in a very squeezing motion.

Aerobic exercise, this type of jog or perhaps a brisk walk, may also help the bloodstream to circulate much better and can assist in improving ED in men who've circulation issues.

Tests

The numerous possible factors behind ED imply that a health care provider will typically request plenty of questions and request blood tests to get performed. Such testing can look for heart disease, diabetes, and reduced testosterone, among other activities. The doctor may also perform a physical assessment, including on the genitals.

Before considering an analysis that requires therapy, a doctor can look for symptoms which have persisted for at the very least 3 months.

Once a health background has been proven, a doctor will undertake further inspection. One simple evaluation, referred to as the 'postage stamp check,' are a good idea in figuring out if the reason is physical instead of psychological.

Men will often have three to five 5 erections a nights. This test assessments for the current presence of erections during the night by finding if postage stamps used round the penis before sleeping include snapped off in a single day. Other exams of nocturnal erection are the Poten ensure that you Snap-Gauge test

GENITAL WARTS INFORMATION, CAUSE AND CHANCE, SYMPTOMS, PROGNOSIS AND TREATMENT

Explanation of Genital Warts

- Are also named venereal warts and so are caused by the herpes virus group, real human papilloma pathogen or HPV.

Description

- This painless, delicate and fleshy expansion normally appears one or two months after coverage, but could incubate so long as nine months.

- Some warts could be so small they could only be determined having a Pap smear.

Causes and Danger Factors

- Genital Warts pass on from contaminated sexual partners.

- Warm moist atmosphere of the vaginal location favors wart expansion.

- Outbreaks might occur during pregnancy and appearance to pass towards the newborn baby.

- Effects clients with defective immune system systems.

- The Man Papilloma Virus is certainly associated with around ninety-percent of cervical malignancies.

- HPV may are likely involved in cancers of this vagina, vulva, penis, and anus.

Symptoms

- Like the majority of STD's (std) genital warts will be painless therefore get unnoticed unless challenging spots develop immediately after exposure.

- HPV may cause an irregular pap smear result

- Women could find vaginal warts round the lips on the vagina, round the anus, and in the vaginal canal.

- Woman may create cervical warts; even lesions unseen in its first stages.

Diagnosis

- Genital warts will be diagnosed by visible examinations

- Colposcopy could be preformed to see the inner reproductive organs in women.

- In some instances a biopsy, taking away a bit of cervical tissue, could be necessary to be able to eliminate an HPV identification.

Treatment

- Chemical treatments which are put on the warts and washed off a long time later.

- Smaller warts my end up being taken away with liquid nitrogen or electrodessication.

SOME SEXUAL DYSFUNCTION AFFECTING WOMEN

Causes and Remedy of Vaginal Dryness

Vaginal dryness indicates lack of dampness in vagina. It generates many issues in sexual pursuits. It creates the sexual intercourse incredibly painful and incredibly less pleasurable. You can find itching and losing sensation while experiencing vaginal dryness and you may first see it during intercourse. Nevertheless the common cause because of this will be menopause but aside from this there's also some other known reasons for vaginal dryness. To be able to get medicine of genital dryness you will need to determine the precise reason. Here are the various leads to and therapy of genital dryness that will help you to stop as a result and treat your trouble.

Causes

o Hormones play a significant role to generate dryness in vagina. The primary reason for genital dryness is loss of estrogen degree in women. The estrogen stage decrease in women because of various explanation including

o Cigarette smoking

o Eradication of ovaries after surgery

o Menopause and Immune system disorder

o Child beginning and Breasts feeding

o Medication during therapy of cancer incorporating chemotherapy and rays therapy.

o Vaginal infection.

o Std

o Diabetes, Major depression and trauma

o Intimate assault and abuse

o Making use of infertility drugs, Harsh dying soaps and perfumes

o Usage of diaphragms and condoms could also lead to this issue because of some allergy.

TREATMENT

Self Care

o Wear Egyptian cotton panties. Proper oxygen circulation will relieve the problem.

o Stay away from soap. Still if you wish to use soap make use of good quality cleaning soap without any fragrance. Perfumed cleaning soap or shampoo can boost your problem.

o Use natural powder of perfume so that it usually do not are exposed to your vaginal region.

o You should use vitamin E engine oil.

o You should use lubricant point out K-Y Jelly. It will help to make your sexual intercourse much less painful.

o Moisturizer may also play an essential role. Single program will reduce the dryness for three days.

Medication

o If self-care approaches do not appropriate your problem you need to take medicine under appointment of doctor.

o If the issue exists because of low degree of estrogen you medical doctor may help you to choose genital estrogen therapy.

o If the issue occurs because of some other causes apart from menopause, your physician can advise you an increased dosage of estrogen engagement ring, estrogen capsule or patches.

Your treating expert may talk to you some private concerns e.g., rape, sexual misuse or domestic assault etc. You need to answer these concerns honestly to your physician which may be very helpful to supply you appropriate treatment. When this happens everything is kept private. After physical evaluation and sexual counselling the treating professional may recommend for a few laboratory ensure that you subsequently begins treatment that involves review of treatment and over-the-counter medicine.

CAUSES OF FUNGUS INFECTIONS

Contrary to popular belief, not only will be these infections a standard difficulty for women, nonetheless it is also popular in men. This sort of infection is normally caused by possessing an extra normal quantity of the fungus Candidiasis on your skin. Normally this fungus infection exists in tiny sums situated in the oral cavity, vagina, skin area and digestive system. In these smaller amounts it usually will not cause sickness or symptoms.

So what brings about Candida albicans to raise and eventually result in outward indications of a yeast infection? Properly there several problems that produce the infection positive that occurs. These conditions are increasingly being pregnant and getting along the way of acquiring antibiotics.

Being pregnant will cause a rise of yeast infection. Why? You have to recognize that your body is certainly going through many alterations and monitoring all the chemical substance improvements in the genital area is quite difficult. Usually through the next trimester of motherhood, the genital secretions that occur will contain much more sugar than typical. The yeast in that case feed on the surplus of sugar which in turn causes the yeast to cultivate until an imbalance with the Candida albicans fungus infection occurs.

The other problem which makes yeast infections ideal to occur is certainly using antibiotics. Some may request why carry out antibiotics cause these kinds of microbe infections. Well although antibiotics destroy the bad germs, they also destroy the good protecting bacteria within you as well. After the protective bacteria is wiped out, an imbalance in the torso occurs that may bring about the Candidiasis fungus to cultivate before infection is rolling out.

SYMPTOMS OF CANDIDA INFECTION

I do recognize that when having the infection, you will see times of discomfort and affliction that's intolerable. A number of the outward indications of this infection are usually itching and losing. Furthermore for men, a rash can seem after possessing sexual intercourse having an infected companion. A burning experience can also happen where the contaminated area feels popular. Also, this sort of infection could cause the infected location to swell and be sore to the touch.

For some which are reading this document, it may because of your first time encountering these symptoms and you also may not be sure you've got a yeast infection. If this is actually the case, i quickly advise that you see a medical expert immediately to make the correct medical diagnosis because there are a few STDs (sexually sent disorders) that undertake similar symptoms. Hence please see a medical expert if you're unsure.

TREATMENTS FOR YEAST INFECTION

The only path to free yourself out of this infection by understanding that lotions along with other over-the-counter ointments will not get rid of the infection in one day. You will in no way cure your yeast infection with ointments, ointments and antibiotics. Essentially a few of these solutions could cause the infection to aggravate and to are more painful. This can be shocking for a few, but should be accepted to be able to remove this agonizing infection.

You intend to recognize that a yeast infection isn't just an "at first glance" issue which may be handled with ointments or other forms of medicines. This infection is basically an internal problem. For this reason superficially dealing with it with some type of cream will surely not get the job done.

HERPES - REASONS AND THERAPY

Herpes simplex, brought on by type 1 infection, primarily spread out by dental secretions and also normally occurring as a concomitant of fever. It may likewise develop in the absence of fever or prior ailment. Herpes simplex infection (HSV) is a virus that usually creates skin infections. There are two types of HSV: HSV kind 1 usually creates little blisters on the mouth, eye, or lips (fever blisters) and also HSV kind 2 normally affects the genital location. Herpes is an infection brought on by 2 various however very closely related viruses.

Reappearances are typically much milder than primary infections as well as are understood frequently as cold sores or high temperature blisters (due to the fact that they might develop during a round of cold or flu). HSV-2 can in some cases create mouth sores.

Genital herpes is normally brought on by HSV-2. Genital herpes is a sexually sent disease. Genital reappearances after the very first outbreak appear to be linked to stress and anxiety, fatigue, lack of sleep, menstruation, and genital friction (brand-new sex-related companion after a time of no sex), although more research study is absolutely needed regarding this subject. Normally reappearances are much more regular in the initial year after the initial outbreak.

Causes

Oral herpes causes chilly sores around the mouth or face.
Oral herpes is an infection created by the herpes simplex
infection. The infection causes uncomfortable sores on your
lips, gum tissues, tongue, roof covering of your mouth, as
well as inside your cheeks.

It is a lot more most likely to take place in individuals over
60 years.

Therapy

Therapy of the infection will certainly depend upon its
extent. Moderate infection is generally treated with topical
and also in some cases dental antiviral drug.

Treatment with acyclovir did not minimize this lasting,
high focus of HSV-2-specific CD4+ T cells at the websites
of healed herpes lesions. Therapy of herpes simplex
keratitis depends upon the extent. A first break out is
typically treated with sometimes oral and also topical antiviral medication. Therapies are readily available to quicken
the healing of the genital sores.

PARAPHILLIA

Paraphilias are emotional disorders specified as sexually exciting dreams, prompts, or habits that are recurring, intense, happen over a period of at the very least six months, as well as create significant distress or disrupt crucial locations of operating.

Except for masochism, medical professionals almost solely identify paraphilias in guys.

There are a variety of different types of paraphilic conditions, each of which has a different emphasis of the patient's sexual stimulation.

There are biological, psychological, and also social risk variables for creating paraphilias.

While the desired sex-related energizer for the paraphilia patient depends upon the details paraphilia, the qualities of the health problem are often extremely comparable, as described in the most existing common recommendation for psychological health diagnoses, the DSM-5.

In order to develop the medical diagnosis of a paraphilia, psychological health experts typically carry out or refer the individual for a medical interview, checkup, as well as routine research laboratory tests. The professional will analyze for any background of psychological health and wellness symptoms.

Treatment of paraphilic sexual problems usually includes the mix of psychiatric therapy and medication.

Paraphilias are fairly chronic, such that a minimum of 2 years of therapy is recommended for also the mildest paraphilia.

Prevention for the advancement of any kind of paraphilic actions normally involves easing the psychosocial threat elements for its development.

What is a paraphilia? What are the various types of paraphilias?

The word paraphilia originates from Greek; para indicates around or beside, and also philia means love. The interpretation of paraphilia is any kind of emotional disorder identified by sexually exciting dreams, urges, or actions that are reoccurring, extreme, happen over a period of at the very least 6 months, and also trigger considerable distress or hinder the victim's work, function, or various other crucial locations of operating. This is rather than sex-related versions, which are sex-related actions that are not typical yet are not a part of any type of ailment.

Numerous people with one of these disorders suffer in secret or silence out of embarassment, and also some engage in sexually offensive actions and also so are invested in not reporting their paraphilia. Women tend to be under-diagnosed with paraphilias, wrongfully offered the advantage of the doubt by those analyzing their sexual actions.

Except for masochism, which is 20 times a lot more common in ladies than men, paraphilias are virtually exclusively detected in men. Lots of individuals that suffer from one paraphilia have even more than one.

According to the most existing standard recommendation for mental illness, the Diagnostic as well as Statistical Guidebook of Mental Disorders, 5th Version (DSM-5), preceded by the DSM-IV as well as DSM-IV-TR, there are a variety of various sorts of paraphilias, each of which has a different emphasis of the patient's sexual stimulation:

• Voyeurism: enjoying an unsuspecting/non-consenting person that is either nude, striping, or participating in sexual activity

• Indecent exposure: exposing one's very own genitals to an unsuspecting person

• Frotteurism: massaging or touching versus a non-consenting individual

• Sexual masochism: being embarrassed, beaten, bound, or otherwise enduring

• Sex-related sadism: the psychological or physical suffering of an additional person

• Pedophilia: sex with a kid that is prepubescent (generally 13 years of ages or younger).

• Fetishism: sex-related attraction with nonliving items or very certain body parts (partialism). Examples of particular fetishisms include somnophilia (sexual stimulation by a person who is unconscious) and urophilia (deriving sex-related pleasure from seeing or thinking concerning pee or urinating).

• Transvestism: cross-dressing that is sexually arousing and also interferes with functioning.

• Autogynephilia is a subtype of transvestism that refers particularly to guys that become excited by thinking or imagining himself as a lady.

• Various other defined paraphilia: some paraphilias do not satisfy complete diagnostic re□uirements for a paraphilic disorder however may have unrestrained sexual impulses that trigger enough distress for the victim that they are identified. Examples of such specific paraphilias include necrophilia (remains), scatologia (obscene phone calls), coprophilia (feces and defecation), and also zoophilia (animals).

Urges to participate in otherwise hostile or coercive sex like rape are not signs and symptoms of a mental illness. Such sex-related offending is as a result ruled out a paraphilia.

WHAT ARE CAUSES AND ALSO THREAT FACTORS FOR PARAPHILIA?

Biological concerns thought to be danger aspects for paraphilias include some differences in brain activity during sexual arousal, as well as general mind structure. Psychological health and wellness professionals have discovered that male pedophiles have lower intelligence scores on psychological screening compared to men who are not pedophiles. Study has also determined that they have a tendency to have a background of making lower □ualities in college than their non-pedophilic e□uivalents, regardless of intellectual capacities as well as finding out designs.

There are a variety of emotional theories about how paraphilias develop. Some see these conditions as a manifestation of jailed psychosexual advancement, with the paraphilic actions defending the individual's psyche against anxiety (defense mechanisms). Others believe paraphilias are the result of the sufferer associating something with sexual stimulation and rate of interests, or by having uncommon very early life sex-related experiences strengthened by having an orgasm. Some view these problems as another kind of obsessive-compulsive disorder.

Mentally, pedophiles who act on their prompts by sexually offending often tend to engage in grossly altered thinking, because they utilize their position of power and also sight upseting as an appropriate way to satisfy their re□uirements, think about children as e□ual sexual beings to grownups, as well as consider their sex-related demands as unmanageable.

An additional theory about paraphilia risk aspects is that they are linked to stages of youth mental development like temperament, early partnership development, injury rep, and interrupted advancement of sexuality, as complies with:

Temperament: a propensity to be extremely inhibited or unchecked with feelings as well as actions

Early partnership formation: a lack of secure self-awareness, difficulty taking care of feelings, and also in seeking assistance and also convenience from others

Injury rep: People that are the target of other or sex-related kinds of misuse, particularly if it occurs during youth, may relate to the abuser such that they act out what was brought upon on them by taking advantage of others somehow. They might likewise act out the trauma by in some way harming themselves.

Interfered with advancement of sexuality: The patterns of what brings one sexual pleasure tend to form by teenage years. People elevated in a house that is either excessively sexually permissive or hindered go to higher risk for developing a paraphilia.

Family members threat aspects for paraphilia advancement consist of high conflict between moms and dads or low supervision by parents, a lack of love from the mother, and also usually not really feeling treated well by their parents. People with paraphilia have a tendency to have trouble making and also keeping close friends and also other relationships.

SEXUAL TRANSFERRED DISEASE

WHAT ARE STDS?

STDs are venereal diseases. This suggests they are frequently-- but not solely-- spread by sexual intercourse. HIV, chlamydia, genital herpes, genital verrucas, gonorrhea, some forms of syphilis, trichomoniasis, and liver disease are STDs.

Sexually transmitted diseases utilized to be called venereal diseases or VD. More than 65 million Americans have an incurable STD.

Sexually transmitted diseases are serious ailments that need therapy. Some Sexually transmitted diseases, such as HIV, can not be healed and also can be lethal. By learning more regarding Sexually transmitted diseases, you can discover ways to protect on your own.

You can obtain a STD from genital, rectal, or foreplay. You can likewise be infected with trichomoniasis through contact with damp or damp items such as towels, damp clothing, or commode seats, although it is more commonly spread out by sexual contact. You are at high risk if:

• You have more than one sex partner

• You make love with someone that has had several partners

• You don't utilize a condom when having sex

• You share needles when injecting intravenous drugs

• You trade sex for money or drugs

You may not recognize you have particular Sexually transmitted diseases up until you have damages to your reproductive body organs (providing you infertile), your vision, your heart, or other organs. Having a Sexually Transmitted Disease may deteriorate the immune system, leaving you more vulnerable to various other infections. If you pass a STD to your newborn child, the baby might experience permanent harm or death.

WHAT TRIGGERS SEXUALLY TRANSMITTED DISEASES?

Sexually transmitted diseases include just about every sort of infection. Microbial STDs include chlamydia, syphilis, and also gonorrhea. Viral Sexually transmitted diseases include HIV, genital herpes, genital excrescences (HPV), as well as liver disease B. Trichomoniasis is caused by a parasite.

The germs that cause STDs hide in sperm, blood, genital secretions, as well as often saliva. Most of the organisms are spread by genital, anal, or foreplay, but some, such as those that cause genital herpes and genital protuberances, may be spread out with skin call. You can get hepatitis B by sharing individual products, such as toothbrushes or razors, with a person that has it.

Sexually Transferred Illness: Myths You Should Watch Out For

Significant strides in clinical study and education and learning have actually unmasked Sexually Transmitted Disease fallacies that will definitely provide mistaken individuals to undesirable repercussions. Although many teenagers and also young people have actually been enlightened concerning these myths, it can always be assumed that there are still some illinformed people. For their details as well as for your suggestion, here are some 5 disproved STD myths.

Misconception:

1. Oral sex guarantees 0% chance of obtaining any sexually transferred disease.

Truth:

2. Just like genital as well as rectal intercourses, oral sex may likewise hand down Sexually transmitted diseases. When there's an open injury in the oral dental caries, this is particularly true. Such injury allows transfer of contaminated blood. For those energetic in sex, even if it's simply dental, STD home test is urged. Undertaking routine

STD test immediately recognizes and also permits the reductions of sending diseases early on.

Misconception:

1. STDs are no suit versus oral contraceptive pills.

Truth:

Oral birth controls or birth control pills were not developed to combat sexually transmitted diseases. Anyone that count exclusively on oral birth control for combating Sexually transmitted diseases is extremely motivated to undertake a scientific or STD house examination.

Misconception:

1. When there's already an episode of sores, Herpes is just infectious.

Fact:

Like most Sexually transmitted diseases, herpes can be transmitted also if the infected individual is not materializing sores and various other particular signs and symptoms. Herpes is a highly transmittable viral disease that can not be reduced by methods that are reliable versus many other Sexually transmitted diseases. Sexually Transmitted Disease examination set for herpes can be bought through the Net.

Misconception:

1. Lack of signs instantly converts to lack of STD.

Reality:

2. This is most definitely among the gravest misconceptions, one can experience concerns to STDs. The success of STDs in contaminating great deals of targets can be extremely attributed to their treacherous nature; they don't let their targets recognize that they're already there.

Many Sexually transmitted diseases, such as Chlamydia, don't have noticeable symptoms. These diseases can only be detected by Sexually Transmitted Disease tests carried out by experienced lab service technicians or through ingenious Sexually Transmitted Disease residence examination packages. Aside from doing not have noticeable signs, a number of Sexually transmitted diseases additionally display symptoms that are often attributed to more common as well as much less alarming medical issues. A clear illustration will be interpreting a situation of bacterial STD gonorrhea as just an ordinary infection of the urinary bladder. It is also worth pointing out that HIV infection only has flu-like signs and symptoms throughout its onset. One might pick from a number of STD test package alternatives for discovering the visibility of HIV before full blown AIDS develops.

Misconception:

1. The human race has currently designed medications for totally eliminating all sorts of STDs.

Truth:

2. Currently, there are still numerous STDs that can't just be healed. Although bacterial STDs can be finished by different anti-biotics, no medicine has actually yet been invented for totally dealing with a large number of virus-caused STDs. The viral infections can just be managed to slightly damaging or safe degrees but the original representative still resides within the victims. For example, herpes infection and also AIDS last a life time. The clinical disaster brought upon by viral Sexually transmitted diseases can be highly credited to their extremely reliable adaptability; medicines that work with them now may no more subdue the infections after a brief while. To quickly minimize what can't be cured, early discovery utilizing Sexually Transmitted Disease test set is a must.

Do Condoms Prevent All Sexually Transferred Conditions?

When they use prophylactics, many of the found out populace feel totally secure in their sex-related relations. Most of the information offered on net as well as elsewhere assert that prophylactics are an effective protection versus HIV/AIDS. Nevertheless, the under-informed masses are not aware of the truth that prophylactics do not provide protection against a number of Sexually Sent Infections (STI) like herpes, HPV, syphilis, pubic lice, or scabies. They spread with skin to skin genital call. Even if no fluid exchange occurs, these STIs might spread out conveniently as well as can create a life threatening problem, no where much less harmful than the much hyped HIV, which make the body immune system weak to the fatal degree.

HIV compromises the immune system by reducing the variety of T-Lymphocytes. The regular variety of T-Lymphocyte is 500 to 1500 which goes down below 200 because of HIV infection. This makes the immune system weak enough for any other pathogen to strike the body and cause secondary infection. Usually, the individual passes away of additional infection triggered by the weakened body immune system that make the body at risk to secondary strikes. These are called opportunist infections, a few of which are pointed out as under:

• Candidiasis of bronchi, throat, esophagus, or lungs

• Intrusive cervical cancer

• Coccidioidomycosis

• Cryptococcosis

• Cryptosporidiosis,

• Cytomegalovirus condition

• Encephalopathy, HIV-related

• Herpes simplex: persistent ulcer(s) (higher than 1 month's duration); or esophagitis, pneumonitis, or respiratory disease

• Histoplasmosis

• Isosporiasis, persistent intestinal tract (more than 1 month's duration).

• Kaposi's sarcoma.

• Lymphoma, several kinds.

• Mycobacterium avium complicated.

• Tuberculosis.

• Pneumocystis carinii pneumonia.

• Pneumonia, reoccurring.

• Progressive multifocal leukoencephalopathy.

• Salmonella septicemia, fre□uent.

• Toxoplasmosis of mind.

• Losing disorder as a result of HIV.

Being a viral infection, antibiotics are useless to stop the infection of HIV. HIV Vaccine, although verified at research study phase is still not offered in free market for masses.

Sexually transferred infections like herpes, HPV, syphilis, pubic lice, or scabies are not stopped with using condoms. So, this is a large misconception among the masses that condoms stop all sexually transferred disease. Additionally, these STIs may lie dormant in the body of the service provider individual with no symptoms or physical indication. Nevertheless, they may transmit the infection to someone who comes in sex-related get in touch with. So, its extremely tough to find effectively that an individual is infected or not.

There are particular misconceptions also concerning sexually transmitted infections. The less severe infection like pubic lice or scabies may transmit by sharing clothing.

Monogamy is the most safe method to avoid any type of sexually transmitted infection as well as prophylactics are not an alternative which could be selected forever.

Below you can do a search to pick the ideal doctor name in your closet door. Our assistance as well as support feel you comfy every time.

VENEREAL DISEASES ROOT CAUSE OF INABILITY TO CONCEIVE.

1. Chlamydia.

It is a type of microorganism that is a Sexually Transmitted Disease that leads to infertility. In males, it creates infection leading to urethritis and conflicts with ejaculation.

2. Epididymitis.

Epididymitis is defined as the inflammation of the epididumis brought on by germs. If infection spreads to the testicles, it is an urinary system infection that leads to the inability to conceive.

3. Gonorrhea.

Gonorrhea is a STD triggered by the bacteria Neisseria gonococcus that leads to epididymitis infection as well as swelling of the uterus in guys, and also the Fallopian tube in ladies. It results in tubal damage creating infertility and also losing the unborn baby.

4. Pyospermia.

Pyospermia is a condition in which high levels of leukocyte exist in the sperm. It is caused by the infection of a Sexually Transmitted Disease someplace in the body. In some cases such infection may create the body immune system acknowledging the sperm as an invader and killing it.

5. Ureaplasma urealyticum.

Ureaplasia urealyticum is a germs belonging to the family Mycoplasmataceae. It is a kind of transmittable bacteria with no symptoms. It is sexually transferred between partners as well as hinders the reproductive procedures including tubal condition, decreases sperm activity as well as the high □uality triggering inability to conceive.

MEDICATIONS FOR STD

HIV/AIDS.

• Nucleoside Opposite Transcriptase Inhibitors.

• abacavir, didanosine (ddl), lamivudine (3TC), stavudine (d4T), zalcitabine (ddC), zidovudine (ZDV).

• Protease Inhibitors.

• indinavir, nelfinavir, ritonavir, sa□uinavir, lopinavir plus ritonavir.

• Nonnucleoside Reverse Transcriptase Inhibitors.

• delavirdine, efavirenz, nevirapine.

• Chlamydia.

• Anti-biotics.

• azithromycin, erythromycin, doxycycline.

• Gonorrhea.

• Prescription antibiotics.

• ceftriaxone, cefixime, ciprofloxacin, ofloxacin.

Gonorrhea and chlamydia can happen in tandem, in which occasion the physician could prescribe a routine of ceftriaxone plus doxycycline or azithromycin.

Pelvic Inflammatory Illness (PID).

Prescription antibiotics.

cefotetan or cefoxitin plus gentamicin, clindamycin plus doxycycline, ofloxacin plus metronidazole.

Usually, two anti-biotics are recommended.

Human Papillomavirus (HPV).

Topical Prep work (creams as well as services that the person uses directly to the afflicted location).

imi□uimod, podophyllin, podofilox, fluorouracil (5-FU), trichloroacetic acid (TCA), interferon.

Genital Herpes.

Antivirals.

acyclovir, famciclovir, valacyclovir.

Syphilis.

Anti-biotics.

penicillin-- doxycycline or tetracycline just if adverse penicillin.

SEX THERAPY

Sex therapy is a type of psychotherapy that addresses mental health issues and/ or emotional concerns affecting a person's sexual function, drive, and/or desire for intimacy.

These issues are typically explored with the help of a licensed sex therapist. Some people seek help individually, while others may pursue sex therapy with a romantic partner.

UNDERSTANDING SEX THERAPY

This specialized form of therapy developed in order to help people address concerns related to sexual intimacy. According to Derek Polonsky, a psychiatrist associated with Harvard Medical School, between 35 and 50 percent of people will experience a long-term sexual issue at some point. Thus, while it may not always be easy to bring up the topic of sexual concerns, they are certainly not uncommon.

Individuals can pursue this type of therapy on their own, whether they are single or in a relationship, or with a partner. While many individuals may find it difficult to talk about sex—especially with a professional they do not know well, while their partner is present—sex therapy can often help couples or individuals gain more confidence, restore or improve sexual health, communicate more effectively, and work on achieving a more fulfilling sex life.

In the early days of sex therapy, it was often considered a tool to help individuals repress various forms of what, at the time, was considered "deviant" sexual behavior. Much has changed in the field since then, and today the approach is often recommended to individuals who have issues with intimacy or couples who are seeking to achieve greater sexual enjoyment. Though the topic of sex may still be considered taboo among many couples or individuals, sex therapy can often help people overcome this aversion and address the topic in productive, helpful ways.

SELECTING A SEX THERAPIST

A sex therapist is a professional psychologist, therapist, social worker, or physician who offers comprehensive counseling services for people dealing with some type of sexual issue.

Certified sex therapists will hold an advanced degree in counseling, therapy, psychology, or related field; achieve a number of hours of sex therapy training and clinical experience; and be credentialed by the American Association of Sexuality Educators, Counselors and Therapists (AASECT). An AASECT certification must be renewed every three years.

Choosing the right therapist will depend on the specific situation of the person/people seeking treatment as well as the therapist's area of expertise. Because certification or licensure for sex therapists has yet to be standardized, it is generally a good idea to ask potential therapists about their professional training in human sexuality and the specific issues they are able to address.

A person who chooses to enter sex therapy individually may be more comfortable discussing sexual issues with a therapist of the same gender. However, all sex therapists are trained to address the emotional, physical, and biological issues that can influence sexual activity in men and women. Many sex therapists also help non-binary, transgender, and intersex people address sexual concerns, but some individuals may find it more helpful to work with a therapist who has experience working with people who are not cisgender. A sex therapist should never attempt to change or deny a person's gender, identity, or sexual orientation, and doing so would be considered a sign of unethical treatment. Further, the issues that bring non-binary, trans, or intersex people to sex therapy may not be in any way related to their identity, and an ethical therapist will not assume this to be the case.

In session, a sex therapist will work to help a person or couple seeking help achieve an improved mental and emotional state in order for them to enjoy a more satisfying sexual experience and/or relationships. Sessions are strictly instructive and verbal, and all exercises and that involve physical contact are performed outside of the session. Sex therapy does not involve having sex with the therapist or being forced to have sexual contact with anyone else. Therapists may, as part of the process, encourage those in treatment to consider participating in certain intimate activities or exercises with their partner, but a person is never made to do so as part of therapy. Sex therapy is largely a mental and emotional reflection of one's own internal conflicts, concerns, and/or □uestions about sex.

WHEN IS SEX THERAPY RECOMMENDED?

In many cases, people participate in sex therapy on a short-term basis (though in some cases, an ongoing or longer-term approach to counseling is needed). A specific treatment plan will rely heavily on the individual needs of the person or couple in therapy.

There are several reasons why a person might choose to seek sex counseling, but it is most often recommended for anyone whose quality of life is affected by their sexual function or desire and/or for anyone having problems with intimacy within a relationship, regardless of age, gender, or background. Adolescents who are confused or concerned about sexual matters may also seek the help of a sex therapist, in some instances.

HOW CAN SEX THERAPY HELP?

Ade□uate and comprehensive sex counseling can have a positive impact on the psychological and sexual health of a person or couple in therapy, even after only a short period of time. Still, the effectiveness of the therapy ultimately depends on the willingness of the person in therapy to accept the concepts presented to them during a session.

Most experts agree that sex therapy—like other modes of therapy—is most helpful when all parties honestly consider the concerns raised and make a considered, collaborative (when applicable) effort to work through them. Most experts agree that sex therapy—like other modes of therapy—is most helpful when all parties honestly consider the concerns raised and make a considered, collaborative (when applicable) effort to work through them.

Sex therapy can be used to address:

- A lack of sexual desire
- Intimacy after infidelity
- A couple's disparity in sex drives
- Intimacy after having children

- Painful intercourse

- A paraphilia, or desire that cause a person distress

- Sex addictions and/or compulsive behavior

- Difficulties achieving orgasm.

Sex therapy is not limited to these issues, but these are some of the most common reasons a person or couple may choose to seek out a □ualified sex therapist.

LIMITATIONS AND CONCERNS OF SEX THERAPY

Because sex can be a controversial subject that may challenge personal values in addition to political and religious views, sex therapy may be difficult for some people. Sex therapists are specially trained to balance their professionalism with these factors in mind, but the effectiveness of sex therapy ultimately depends on the quality of the therapeutic relationship and on the goals and motivation of the person or couple in therapy. One or more of these factors may be compromised by the person in therapy's belief system, which is why it is important for individuals to carefully select a sex therapist they feel comfortable with.

CONCLUSION

If you want to see, your partner jump your bones often like he or she utilized to do in those very early days, initially ensure that you are mentally connected with your partner. Little points like a periodic present of a flower bouquet or sexy underwear can make your companion feel sitting pretty. All these can pave the method to complete emotional satisfaction, which might better lead you to sexual satisfaction related features..

Do not go yet; One last thing to do

If you enjoyed this book or found it useful I'd be very grateful if you'd post a short review on it. Your support really does make a difference and I read all the reviews personally so I can get your feedback and make this book even better.

Thanks again for your support!

9 7 9 8 7 4 6 2 1 4 8 6 7